Boots on the Stairs

Boots on the Stairs

ROBIN JAYNE DEDEKER

Boots on the Stairs© copyright 2013 by Robin Jayne Dedeker; all rights reserved. No part of this book may be reproduced in any form whatsoever, by photography or xerography, or by any other means, by broadcast or transmission, by translation into any kind of language, nor by recording electronically or otherwise, without permission in writing from the author, except by a reviewer, who may quote brief passages in critical articles or reviews.

Softcover/Paperback ISBN:
ISBN-13: 978-1490919218
ISBN-10: 149091921X
Book design and typesetting: Robin Jayne Dedeker
Cover Art Design Idea: Robin Jayne Dedeker
Cover Art Creation: Brent S. Duncan and Robin Jayne Dedeker
First Printing 2013

17 16 15 14 13   5 4 3 2 1

To order visit www.MomentsOfIntuition.com

Contents

7   Dedicated with Love

9   Knock, Knock! (a poem)

11 Introduction

13 Chapter One: *Boots on the Stairs*

33 Chapter Two: *Just-A-Swingin'*

61 Chapter Three: *Politics As Usual*

89 Chapter Four: *Once Upon a Time*

109 Chapter Five: *The King and I*

161 Chapter Six: *Expiration Dates*

199 Chapter Seven: *Out of the Mouths of Babes*

225 Acknowledgements

229 About the Author

231 About the Cover Art

233 Available Books

Dedicated with Love

To my Higher Power, whom I call God, for pushing me in those times when I need it, and for accepting that I am not perfect, while always loving me unconditionally.

To all of the angels, spirit guides, and the spirits of all of our loved ones, who work tirelessly to bring messages of guidance, hope, and unconditional love to all.

To my husband, Robert (Bob) Dedeker, for listening to me whenever I need a friendly ear, and for hugging me in those times when some of my spirit connections touch me deep in the heart.

To Huck Finn, our Jack Russell rough coat terrier dog. Huck worked hard to get to heaven so that he could begin his spirit's healing.

And to my son, Brady's spirit, who keeps knocking at my door.

Knock, Knock!
(A poem)

Knock, Knock! Who's there?
It's me, the spirit of the person who just appeared as a visual image within your own spirit's mind, in the place we also call the third eye.
How can I see you in my mind's eye, knocking on my door? You died; I attended your funeral and placed flowers at your grave!

Only my Earthly body died and that is all that you saw lying in the casket, so still and so reserved. If you had not focused so much on only what you can see with your physical eyes you might have noticed me, standing aside you in spirit, one arm around you to comfort you, and the other arm reaching out to the heavens as God held *my* hand to comfort me.

Why would *you* need our Higher Power to comfort you? Does your spirit feel pain, or grief, or joy? Do you still hear the music that you so loved to play on your guitar and on my piano? Hey, does God allow you to make beautiful music in heaven? Oh my! I have so many questions that I want answers for—can *you*, my loved one, provide me with all that I need?

The Universe is there to comfort each one of us, at all times, and in the ways that we truly need, so that we can learn and grow as his spirit children. Yes, I feel all of the same emotions that you do, even in heaven, because all that I ever was, is still who I am. My physical body was merely my transportation through the life path that I just completed.

Music will always be important to my spirit's heart, as I am a spirit who chooses to heal primarily through the vibrations of music. And as I continue to make music from the other side of the veil, my intentions are to help others who also heal through musical vibrations of energy.

God sent me here, to open the door to your conscious mind, so that you can begin to get all of those burning questions answered. The Universe knows that *you* are a spirit, a person, who heals with knowledge. It is only through your willingness to stay open in your spirit's heart, thinking mind, and physical body that will you be able to receive the knowledge that will become wisdom that will help others heal, too.

—Robin Jayne Dedeker
February 1, 2012

Introduction

Life as a gifted psychic medium is filled with moments that are so extraordinary that it sometimes feels as though I must take a seat, just to catch my breath. On the other hand, my life also includes all of the mundane chores and activities that most others have to deal with such as laundry, grocery shopping, and cleaning the bathroom. In the way that only the Universe can achieve, I often find that the two extremely different components of my life will meld together to create unforgettable moments. In those times when boring life chores collide with psychically charged spirit connections, I try not to miss the opportunities to learn, and to grow, as a spiritual being and as a psychic medium. That said, I am also a person who has a busy life. A life in which I am required to work hard at maintaining some level of positive balance within all of the roles I play. As a result, there are occasions when a spirit has to work harder to gain my attention.

As a woman of fifty-eight years, I have often found that the Universe, whom I call God, seems to have great expectations of me; so, too, does my spirit within. I have always held myself to fairly high standards—in all things that I take part in—and feel a deep need to keep learning throughout my entire lifetime. I have also come to recognize that my Higher Power has placed me into a life path upon which I am meant to teach others about many things, including, but not limited to, that which pertains to psychically gifted persons, such as myself. It is in that spirit of teaching others that I find myself drawn to writing books in which I can teach others about psychic mediums, and their abilities, through the simple action of sharing some of my own psychic moments in life.

For you, my readers, this book is meant to be an insightful look at the real life of a psychically gifted woman, wife, mother, grandmother, friend, and businesswoman, with the focus on psychic interactions and spirit connections. All of the psychic experiences that I have chosen to share with you are told from my own unique perspective, and in the order in which I have felt intuitively guided to place them within my book.

It is not necessary for my readers to be psychically gifted in order to gain insight from this book. It has been my personal experience that we read whatever books we are meant to read, at any given time, in our lives. The purpose and importance for any person to read about my psychic connections to the Universe, to angels, spirit guides, and even to the spirits of loved ones—yours and mine—will always be revealed when it is time in the universe. But for now, sit back and enjoy the read, as I help the Universe to "lift the veil" for a peek inside my psychic world!

CHAPTER ONE

Boots on the Stairs

My name is Robin Jayne Dedeker and I call myself a psychic medium for two reasons: The first is that I was blessed with many psychic gifts that allow me to connect with the spirits of all beings. Consequently, I can act as a medium, or the "go-between" person, whenever the Universe requires a message from any spirit to be passed on to another person who is still living an Earthly life. The second reason I call myself a psychic medium is because that is the name—the title if you will—that God told me about during one of my private tune-in sessions with him. It was in the fall of 2002 that I first became totally, consciously, aware of the ability that I have to connect directly to our Higher Power. That was an inspiring event that helped me to better comprehend the innate gift that each of us has within our inner selves. I learned that our intuition is what gives each of us a direct line of communication to the Universe, to a Higher Power that I call "God."

In short, I asked God what I should call myself as I went forward in my life path to do the work he had been guiding me to do. God answered, *"You are a psychic medium and that is what you should call yourself."* I saw no reason to doubt our Higher Power; the words I heard resonated as truth within my spirit. I made a choice, in those very moments, to honor that title to the best of my abilities as I move along the life path that God placed me upon, so many years ago.

I was born in 1954 and raised in the Twin Cities region of Minnesota. I have been aware of spirit visits for as long as I can remember, though I did not think of myself as psychically gifted for many years. My own birth family was not psychically gifted so the topic of spirits, ghosts, or psychic abilities, never came up at our dinner table. But I have long since learned that those of us who have psychic abilities often view the things that we sense as "normal" because that is who we are and we don't have any other way to relate to "how" we perceive the world. It is what it is, nothing more and nothing less.

While I cannot speak for any other psychically gifted person, I know that my psychic gifts were open from the moment I was born into this life. I grew up psychically "normal" yet, blissfully unaware that I was truly gifted. In this way, I believe that God allowed me to live the first forty-six years of my life in the way that most people tend to live. Humankind has long had the tendency to pay more attention to that which can be perceived through the five physical senses of sight, sound, feeling, taste, and smell, while we often push away, dismiss, or ignore spirit connections.

My personal "normal" did, however, include the awareness that the intuition within me was strong since childhood. The proof of that was constantly being revealed to me, in nearly every aspect of my life. I am a person who believes that every living Being contains powerful intuition within his or her inner self/spirit. Unfortunately, we have long pushed away those internal gut instincts because society has not taught us to respect or to nurture them. Our

Higher Power, angels, spirit guides, and the spirits of our loved ones have all worked hard to guide us, no matter what our Earthly education has provided to us thus far. That said, the time has come for open, respectful conversation and education about intuition.

∞

Beyond intuition, there is another level of spiritual gifts that, I believe, our Creator has infused within some individual spirits that allow many different ways by which spirit connection is possible. These are the gifts I refer to as "psychic abilities." It is through the many psychic moments, and spirit encounters, that I have personally experienced, that I have come to know that I am psychically gifted.

The very nature of psychic abilities lends itself to an aura of mystery and intrigue, as well as some people express a fear of psychically gifted people. As a result, a large part of my life path involves educating and enlightening others through my books and my psychic work. I believe the best way to teach about any subject is to explain things in such a way as to allow others to better relate to any given situation, so that is how I write. Additionally, in an effort to keep things flowing easily, I have included, in my book, descriptions of psychic terms to explain my abilities in the simplest way possible.

I have come to know that many psychics refer to these gifts with words such as clairvoyance, clairaudience, clairsentience, and so forth, but my intuition has always led me to recognize that most everything can be understood by the masses if only we are willing to look at things through the lens of simplicity. With that in mind, I try to keep my work and my writing as psychically simple as possible. That said, you probably would not ever read the words "clairvoyance, clairaudience, or clairsentience" anywhere else in this book.

I tend to think of my psychic gifts as extensions of the five normal senses that each of us are born with, whether all of those senses work well or not. In other words, if I say that I can "see" a spirit it means exactly what you think it means—*I saw a spirit who presented itself to me in some way that allowed me to get a visual sense of him or her.* Of course that means that if I have written that I "heard" a spirit you can be certain that I mean, "*I actually heard a spirit talk to me through some form of verbal communication.*" It would only follow that any references I make to the other three senses—feeling, smelling, and tasting—all mean exactly what they say.

Simplicity is the key to understanding everything and I use that same code of communication with any spirit that the Universe allows me to connect with. It doesn't matter how intelligent a person or spirit is, I have discovered that the best way to communicate anything in life is to break it down to its most basic form. Keep in mind that does not mean that everything can be explained in just a few words, or in words that a young child could always understand, because some topics do require deep thinking. But in developing a good, solid base for learning about psychic and spiritual connections, I believe it is always good to start with the basics and then allow each person to dive in as deep as he or she feels comfortable with.

All of this talk about "keeping it simple" brings to mind a couple of psychic experiences that occurred in the winter of 2004 that brought me to a deeper level of spiritual understanding through the simple spirit connections that can take place in any of our lives. The key is to keep oneself open to the wonders and the learning process that all spirit connections can bring to each of us. We must also accept the fact that most—but not all—spirit experiences occur because someone we know has died, in the physical sense, and his or her spirit has returned home to heaven, to rest and to heal.

Losing our loved ones to death is a natural part of the circle of life, and it helps tremendously when we can reach a level of spiritual understanding that allows us to accept death in that way. Yet death is not the end of our connection to the spirits who have resided within the physical bodies of those we have known. It has been my personal experience that the Universe allows many of the spirits who have left this Earth to visit from time-to-time. Not only do those visits help those spirits to heal, but it can significantly assist in the process of healing from the grief of loss for those who are left to go on living Earthly lives.

∞

My father-in-law, Roger, died in February 2004, after spending nearly three years in a nursing home facility. He had suffered a stroke about fifteen years prior to his death, which had resulted in the entire left side of his body becoming paralyzed. Roger was a large, heavy, man, so to live life with only the use of one side of his body had been difficult for him and for his caregivers. The bulk of the responsibility for Roger's care had fallen on his wife, Eunice, who was a small woman of slight build.

Additionally, my husband, Robert (Bob) Dedeker, had personally taken on many roles that his father could no longer fulfill due to the paralysis caused by his stroke. For many years Bob cared for his parents' lawn, shoveled their driveway and sidewalks throughout the long Minnesota winters, and dutifully handled the difficult task of transporting his now-handicapped father to many doctor appointments or physical therapy at the Minnesota Veteran's Hospital.

I did not personally know Roger before his stroke as I met and married his son, Bob, in 1994, but I did get to know my father-in-law pretty well before his death at the age of seventy-seven years. Many times I found myself assisting Bob in the chores required that allowed his parents to stay living in their home near us in Shakopee, Minnesota. Grocery shopping seemed to be a never-ending task as we would shop for our own large, combined family, and then a couple of days later, we would be back at the store with a long list from Eunice to accommodate the needs of her and her husband.

Bob and I often shared the task of loading his father up in a car. With Roger's wheelchair collapsed and stored in the trunk, we ventured out to give Roger opportunities to socialize, while offering Eunice a much-needed break from constant care giving. In as much as we recognized Roger's need to get out of the house, and for Eunice to have time to herself, there were many times when we would first remove several inches of snow, from a long section of Roger's yard, just so that we could pull our car up close to his home for wheelchair accessibility.

Snow removal frequently consumed our nights and weekends. Through the long Minnesota winters we took care of our home as well as Bob's parents' home, often leaving us too exhausted to enjoy life. We both had full-time jobs and obligations to meet with our combined total of five teenage sons. We were also homeowners and had all of the responsibilities that go along with keeping our own home and yard in decent shape. Needless to say, my husband and I felt overwhelmed, and too often, unappreciated.

Occasionally two of our five sons, Brady or Brent, would lend a hand with Roger's care. Brent's wife, Amanda, pitched in to help Eunice care for Roger, during the last year he lived at home, before he was transferred to a professional nursing care facility. Now and then Roger and Eunice's other four children, and their family members, stepped in to help. But for many years, Bob took on the lion's share of assisting his mother, in the care of his father.

As any caregiver comes to know, the stress and strain of filling the needs of a person who can no longer care for him or herself can be overwhelming. There comes a time when even the most well meaning family members must acknowledge their personal limitations. For Bob, and for me, that time came into sharp focus in the spring of 2002; the time when we both knew we could no longer give so much of ourselves to the care of Roger and Eunice Dedeker.

My son Brady had committed suicide on December 31, 2000, and the resulting grief and healing process seemed to fill all of our time, save for the hours we spent at our full-time jobs. Although Bob continued to try to assist his mother in the care of his father, he could no longer carry that load. Through the guidance of his own strong intuition, Bob made the decision to let his four siblings and their spouses step in to fill the needs that he and I had taken on for so long. God's guidance was clear and strong. Bob was left with the full understanding that, while *we* had learned much and grown spiritually through the action of care giving for his parents, it was time to let others live and learn by caring for Roger and Eunice, within the context of their specific and unique life paths.

You might wonder "why" I have shared the story of Roger and Eunice's care, after he was paralyzed, in my book about psychic connections. The answer is simple: The relationships we foster in life help to determine the quantity and the quality of the future spirit connections that the Universe allows us to experience. We tend to experience spirit communications with those whom we have fostered a strong and positive connection during our lifetimes. In the case of my father-in-law, Roger, both my husband and myself had worked hard to develop as open and strong of a level of communication as possible while Roger was still in his Earthly life. As you will soon learn, the relationships we each had with Roger were important in setting the scene for a couple of amazing spirit connections, just days after Roger's death.

∞

Roger Dedeker died peacefully in the early morning hours of February 19, 2004, just as most people were starting the day. Roger was a man who liked to control as much of his life as possible, even from his long-time seat in a wheelchair. He had kept his business and personal affairs in order, right up to the time of his death. In that way, his family had little to do other than to plan his funeral, per his specifications, and to be in attendance.

Like most families, the members of the extended Dedeker family do not all view life or death from the same perspective. With Roger's death, I tried hard to respect that and did not impose my psychic or spiritual views upon them. However, that did not stop the Universe from "opening up the veil" to the Other Side during Roger's funeral visitation. Yes, indeed, there was a great deal of spirit activity in that funeral home, to the point where it became overwhelming to me. In one instance, during the funeral visitation, I felt I had to sit down. I needed to sit quietly so that I could think about all that I was seeing, hearing, and feeling, within the funeral home setting.

I sat down upon a metal folding chair in the front row of the funeral home's visitation room that had been assigned to Roger O. Dedeker. My chair was located directly to the right of where my son, Brent, had already seated himself. Brent was twenty-seven years old at that time and is also in possession of some strong psychic abilities.

Mother and grown son to one another, daughter-in-law and step-grandson to Roger, we sat quietly, lost in our own thoughts about Roger's life and his death. Suddenly I gasped and Brent said, "Did you see that, Mom?" I turned to look at Brent and saw that he had a big grin on his face. I knew that *he* had seen the same thing that I had just witnessed—Roger's spirit had just wheeled himself in a "spirit wheelchair" straight through the open coffin that held his now-deceased physical body! And as if that wasn't shocking enough, Roger's spirit turned its head in our direction and gave us a big smile!

I could no longer hold back the smile that now filled my face. I knew my son and I had just been witness to a wonderful spirit connection that only God can allow. My heart felt happy and at peace for Roger, yet I felt as though I could not wait to be out of that funeral home. It was the same place that my son, Brady, had been eulogized after his death, and there was just too much emotion and energy coming at me. That feeling continued the next day when we returned to attend Roger's funeral service, also held at the funeral home. The mixture of positive energy from the dead, mixed with so much negative energy from the grief of the living, was simply too much for me to bear.

I knew as I exited that funeral home that my Higher Power was letting me know that I would not be attending many more funerals in my lifetime. The level of my psychic abilities gives me countless opportunities to see, hear, feel, taste, and even to smell every little bit of spirit activity that God allows. All of that is wonderful, but I have also grown spiritually since Brady's death. I truly believe that "the spirit lives" and have had much proof of that concept. I do not view death in the same, traditional way in which I was raised.

I learned through Roger's death, and the funeral process that followed, that I no longer need that right of passage that a funeral provides in my life. Rather I *need* the spirit connection that follows and can take place anywhere, and at any time, that God chooses.

I know that I do not personally have to be in a funeral home, a cemetery, or in close proximity to the physical body of a deceased person, in order to have a connection with his or her spirit. I have only to remain strong in my faith that our Higher Power will provide all that each of us needs for our personal spiritual growth, including, but not limited to, proof of spirit.

The deaths of our loved ones can, at times, feel like poorly timed events. I have come to understand that everything in life—including death—is actually timed to a sense of perfection that only our Creator can orchestrate and have full knowledge of. In the case of my father-in-law, it felt to me as though Roger's spirit was ready to go, as he was weary of a life lived in confinement.

Roger was a man who enjoyed socializing. He tried hard to remain upbeat and cheerful in a nursing home setting, which is not always easy to do. But if his spirit seemed ready, his mind was not. It appeared to me that my husband's father was a person who longed for more time on this Earth to spend with his large extended family. That said, his physical body was simply worn out.

Knowing Roger as I did, I fully expected his spirit to try to make a connection with Bob from the Other Side. I was also accepting of any spirit communication that he might make with me as well. I have learned that there is no way to determine when, or even if, the spirit of anyone we know might attempt to communicate with us so it is best to leave it up to our Higher Power. Again, everything happens in the perfect timing of the Universe and we will notice that if we follow our personal sense of intuition.

∞

Roger's funeral was held on Monday, February 23, 2004, and soon after Bob and I found ourselves returning to the mundane routines of life. It is often those daily routines that help a person to feel useful, especially after the death of a loved one. Bob returned to his job as a painter in the maintenance department of a large school district and I returned to work out of my home as a psychic medium.

A few days after Roger's funeral I felt the need to do some laundry. I sorted the dirty clothes into piles and then loaded up our laundry baskets. The date was Thursday, February 26, 2004, and the time was approximately 8:30 a.m. (CST).

Our laundry is done in the basement of our home. That area of our home is accessed from a back door within our kitchen. Carrying a heavy basket of laundry in my arms, I made my way to the rear kitchen door. I shifted the laundry basket to my right hip; that allowed my left hand to go free so that I could open the door.

As I swung the door open I found myself quickly grabbing for the stair railing, trying hard to steady myself on the first step. Normally I would have simply kept walking down the first four steps, reached a small landing, turned to the left, and preceded down seven more steps. That would bring me to the basement level of our home. To my surprise, I could not proceed down the steps because there were boots on the stairs . . . boots *everywhere!*

I steadied myself by grabbing the handrail and then turned to set the laundry basket down on the kitchen floor. Turning my attention back to the stairway full of boots, I quickly became confused. Small boots, large boots, and medium sized boots, had been placed randomly all about the stairs. Black boots, brown boots, and even a few pairs of little, pink, "girly" boots lay upon our basement stairs.

I knew that those pink boots belonged to our three young granddaughters, Autumn, Gillian, and baby Mara. At that time in our lives, my son Brent, his wife Amanda, and their three young daughters, were living in the basement apartment portion of our home, however, we did not share that stairway. To access the basement apartment they would enter through a separate, rear, walkout door. That door leads into the house from the driveway, via the back alley.

The apartment door also leads into its own entryway, and it is within that entryway that Brent, and his family, stored their hats, gloves, mittens, shoes, and boots. Amanda had special boot trays upon which her family placed their winter boots to dry. That routine had never varied. Bob and I stored our boots in the laundry area of our basement, upon boot trays of our own.

As I made my way down the steps, I found it best to hold tight to the handrail. Those boots were staggered all over the steps, preventing a person from walking up or down easily. I was bewildered by the display of "boots on the stairs." I began to wonder if someone was playing a trick on me, though I knew no one in our family home really fit the description of a practical joker or trickster.

I shrugged my shoulders, perplexed, and deep in my own thoughts, when I suddenly remembered I had to get some laundry done. I began grabbing the nearest boots and returning them to the boot trays where they belonged. As I did that I was struck by the fact that there were two pairs of heavy, brown, rubber boots with liners that belonged to Bob and to Brent that someone had gone to great lengths to set upon different steps. One boot here, another there, and a really heavy one all the way up at the top of the stairway by the kitchen door. Hmmm, that seemed quite strange. I never heard anyone making noise on the stairway. I also knew that Bob hadn't put those boots there, because he typically left for work by 6:30 in the morning, with no time to spare. And besides, my conscious mind knew he would never try to trip me up on the stairs. I was still recovering from severe back pain caused by the grief from my son Brady's death. No person that lived within our home space would try to harm me by placing boots on those stairs. My intuitive sense allowed me to feel there was another reason for this display of boots all over our basement stairs.

With all of the boots returned to their proper storage places, I resumed my laundry chores and made a mental note to ask Bob about the boots later that night. As my day progressed, I gave the whole incident no further thought. I was kept busy with my job and personal obligations. Night came, and Bob returned home from a busy day of painting. However, the topic of "boots on the stairs" never came up. Instead, we settled in to watch a program on the television, before going to bed.

∞

The next morning I awoke with the thought in my head that I needed to go downstairs and visit with Brent and his family. My intuition is strong, and I do pay close attention to it. I knew there had to be a special reason "why" I was getting that recurring thought to *"Get downstairs and visit with Brent and his family!"*

Within a half hour or so I was dressed and ready to go downstairs. I reached for the phone and called Brent, wanting to make sure they were up, and ready for a visitor. It was nearly 10 o'clock in the morning, yet I had not taken time to fix myself anything to eat. It was a pleasant surprise when Brent answered the phone and invited me for an impromptu breakfast. I happily accepted my son's offer. *"This is feeling like a very good day!"* I thought to myself, as my hand turned the knob on the kitchen door. I swung the door wide open, expecting that I would be able to walk down the basement steps.

To my utter amazement, the stairway was—once again—filled with boots! I laughed out loud! Someone was clearly trying to get my attention by playing that prank; I was going to get to the bottom of it! I was glad that I was going downstairs to visit with Brent, Amanda, and our three granddaughters. I couldn't wait to share the "boots on the stairs" story with them. Once again, holding tight to the stair railing, I made my way carefully down the basement steps and walked into the apartment area.

Brent and his family have always enjoyed sleeping in later than Bob and I tend to, and I could see from their faces that they hadn't been up long. I wondered if any of them were responsible for the boot prank, but kept it to myself for a while longer. I watched each one closely as they were getting ready for breakfast. My hope was that the prankster would do something to reveal him or herself.

After breakfast I asked Brent, Amanda, and the girls, to accompany me to the other side of the basement. My intuition told me it was time for them to see all of those boots on the stairs. However, upon seeing that display of boots, I could see from their faces that Brent and Amanda were as puzzled as I was. The little ones seemed confused, and then appeared to be a little bit scared, as they wondered aloud, "Who would take our boots, Grandma Robin?"

It was clear to me that the answer to all of those boots being strategically placed on the rear, interior, stairway of our home was not yet being revealed to me. I said goodbye to Brent and his family, and once again, began removing all of those boots and returned them to their proper boot trays.

When that task was completed I felt the strongest urge to call my husband, Bob, at his work, to discuss my strange encounters with so many boots on the stairs. It was nearly time for his scheduled lunch at his employer so I grabbed my telephone and dialed his number, happy to hear his voice as he answered my call.

My husband knows that I am not a woman or a wife who bothers her spouse at work for trivial, daily occurrences. Bob listened carefully as I explained what I had encountered on those back steps of our home for the past two days. Suddenly he broke his silence and interrupted me with, "Robin—*I've have found boots all over the stairs for the past two mornings when I left for work at 6:30 a.m.! What the heck is going on?*"

Needless to say Bob's words elicited a wave of energy that ran through my entire body—the kind of energy rush I get from my spirit or from God when something "rings true" to me. That rush of energy held strong as Bob continued to explain that he had also taken the time to put all of those boots back onto their respective boot trays, both on our side of the basement, and in the entry way of the apartment area. Bob hadn't wanted me to trip over all of those boots if I had tried to walk down the stairs without the light on or while carrying laundry. Just as I had experienced *my* personal encounter with many boots on the stairs of our home for the past two days, so, too, had

Bob. Neither of us had realized that the other person was also being given the opportunities to experience this phenomenon with the very boots that protect the feet of each family member who currently lived in our large home. We were both feeling a strong sense of excitement as I asked the Universe, whom I call God, to "Please tell us who is responsible for all of those boots on the stairs!"

I listened and watched carefully through my psychic senses, but I only saw God smile as he brought my son Brady's spirit in to connect with me. I laughed as I "saw" Brady's spirit eyes twinkle with amusement when I asked him, "Brady, did *you* move all of those boots onto the stairs for us to see?"

"Nope, it wasn't me, Mom!" I heard Brady's spirit say, but he indicated that he could not explain further. I was thoroughly stumped and confused—when suddenly the image of my father-in-law's spirit came into view. I "saw" my husband's father, Roger, through the help of my third eye, within my spirit's mind. Roger spirit was smiling and happy as he revealed himself to me in spirit. I psychically "saw" him—just as I had seen him so many times during his life—a large, elderly man confined to a wheelchair, by the paralysis caused by a stroke.

But in the next instant I "saw" Roger's spirit as a much younger and stronger man, one who appeared to be in his mid-late twenties. He stood tall and did not require the aid of a wheelchair. The strength of his younger self had returned to him after his physical body had died, now just eight days prior. Roger's spirit was joyful as he explained that it was *him* who had moved all of those boots—large and small—repeatedly onto the rear, interior, stairway of our home. Roger's spirit's energy was ecstatic that God had allowed him to prove to Bob, and to me, that while his Earthly life ended, he was no longer suffering from paralysis in his spirit. Beginning just seven days after his death, Roger's spirit had already been capable of moving Earthly objects, some of them quite heavy for a newly crossed spirit to transport. Just *one* of Bob's heavy winter boots weighed in at 2.5 pounds! Roger's spirit had moved many boots, many times, and had placed them individually in random order so that they covered that entire stairway!

I really do not know who was more excited at all that had been revealed—Roger's spirit, Bob, or myself. All three of us knew that this was more than God allowing another spirit to reveal themselves to us, in some way. No, this was powerful proof that the limitations that may affect us during our Earthly lives can be lifted, as we join our Higher Power in the Light, and as our spirits choose to heal! My spirit, mind, and body were filled with such a positive affirmation of what the Universe had allowed Roger's spirit to be a part of, as a way to further assist in our spiritual growth. For a brief moment, everything seemed to stand perfectly still.

Suddenly I was brought back into the moment as I heard Bob's voice crack with emotion; I realized that I, too, could barely speak without tears. It was clear to both of us that we would never become complacent about the miraculous and amazing spirit encounters that the Universe chooses to share with us. Each one is so extraordinary and so important that it could stand alone as a life changing moment. Even if that one spirit encounter were all a person was ever allowed to experience, it would be invaluable for one's spiritual growth.

∞

Bob and I have been blessed to have frequent spirit encounters and interactions through the very life paths we are guided to walk upon. And my work as a psychic medium and author seems to open the veil between the Earthly plane of existence and the heavens ever wider, every day. I feel blessed to live a life that is so amazing, and yet, so psychically simple.

You might wonder if God ever allowed Roger's spirit to connect with Bob or myself again; the answer is yes. There have been a few psychic conversations during which my husband's father has spoken to me, or has "shown" me a brief vision, all of which I have passed on to Bob. I am also aware of a couple of times when Roger visited Bob, or myself, in spirit during the course of dreams that we have had. That said, none of these connections has ever come close to the time his spirit placed those boots on the stairs.

While I cannot speak for my husband, Bob, I know that I have never been able to look at any of the winter boots—lined up on the plastic boot trays in our basement—without thinking of Roger and feeling his spirit's joy again. In that way, I urge you to pay close attention to all of the signs in your own life. You never know when, or in what ways, a spirit may make its presence known to you, and the deeper meaning behind any visit. Embrace those moments of spirit connections and stay open to a life of psychic simplicity! The spiritual growth that results within you will bring you great inner peace and a sense of abounding joy.

CHAPTER TWO

Just-A-Swingin'

There are two things that my inner child loves to do; one is to sit on a swing and allow myself to completely relax, the other is to spend time getting to know the children in my life. The latter is accomplished by simply *listening* to those children as they describe all that life and the Universe is allowing them to experience. In spite of the fact that I am a grown woman with a husband, adult children, and several grandchildren, I never tire of the opportunities that God gives me to enjoy swinging, and any words of wisdom that come from children I know or meet.

Swinging on a homemade wooden swing, attached to my Grandma Laura's clothesline pole, was a fairly common occurrence when I was a small child. My parents routinely brought my four sisters and I to visit my maternal grandparents at their home in St. Paul, Minnesota. Those visits took place on a weekly basis over the course of many years. I loved to go to my grandparents' home as it always felt like a place where children were welcome, and that feeling was generally accompanied by a smile and a hug!

As a young child, I felt that I could trust my grandparents, something that has followed through in my life as a grandparent. I try hard to convey that same trust to my grandchildren. I want my grandchildren to know that I will always love them, no matter what God has in store for them to experience as they grow up. Life and the Universe has already taught me that there is much good that will come into a person's life, but there will also be some challenges that we may perceive as "bad." Other life experiences can only be described as downright "ugly." In that way, our children and our grandchildren cannot be kept from living his or her life, compete with all of the spiritual lessons and growth, but they do need loving and trustworthy adults to lean on from time to time.

As adults, most of us have begun to figure out that life can be difficult, and at times, we need to rely upon others to help us master a new skill. Those things also apply to children as the Universe begins to test us and teach us from the moment we are born. I discovered quite early in my life that the childhood activity of swinging was one way in which the Universe taught me many things.

As most young children require, I, too, needed a trusty adult in my life who would spend time helping me to master the physical dexterity and skills necessary to move a swing forwards and backwards. If you have ever tried to teach a young child "how" to swing on their own, you already know that the body mechanics that take place as a person is swinging can be somewhat difficult to explain to a child. There is more to swinging that just seating yourself upon the swing itself as a person certainly cannot "will it" to move back and forth on its own.

Thanks to the patience and tenacity of a few loving adults in my life, I was able to master the art of swinging at a very young age. I have vivid memories of running to that sturdy, wooden swing that my Grandpa Bud had made for his grandchildren, and using all of the strength I could muster, I found that I could get myself seated upon that swing. With my two small hands gripping the ropes on either side of me, I would move my body in the rhythmic way that only one who is serious about his or her swinging could really understand. The upper body must shift itself back and forth in such a way as to propel the swing in either a forward or backward direction, while at the same time anticipating *just the right moment* to shift itself in the opposite direction, thus increasing the momentum.

Of course, those among us who, in our youth, took swinging to an art form, also know that the knees and legs play a powerful role in allowing any swing to achieve maximum altitude. "Pump your legs!" is a phrase that is commonly heard, at any playground, whenever a child is about to embark on his or her inaugural solo flight on the mighty swing set! Proud parents and grandparents do not sit on the sidelines, but seem to be drawn ever closer to the swing upon which their young loved one is seated. Smiles abound and the energy becomes infectious, as no bystander is unaffected whenever another child learns how to master the art of swinging.

I find myself smiling, even now as I type the words of my story, for there is a freedom that comes with the very action of swinging that nearly defies explanation. Swinging is not just about mastering a complex set of physical actions simultaneously, but, I believe, it also gives us the chance to "leave this Earth," if only for a moment or two. Once our feet leave the ground to begin the process of pumping rhythmically, and the shifting of our upper body has been activated, we find that our arms have grown stronger and our little hands seem to "know" that they cannot let go for we have achieved lift-off!

As we continue to swing, the laws of gravity that hold our physical bodies here on Earth, are still in place. And yet, it feels as though we are defying gravity, albeit an illusion. Even as a young child we quickly learn that, "What goes up, must come down!" Logically speaking, we *know* that gravity still binds us to the Earth, but that does not stop our spirits, minds, and bodies from soaking up every single opportunity that swinging provides to us.

Swinging is a great workout for the physical body and can be an amazing way to relax the conscious mind. If done in a positive setting, swinging can truly bring a person to a level of relaxation that is akin to self-hypnosis. In this way, a child can easily connect his or her inner self (spirit) to the intuitive guidance of the Universe, of God. It is through this same process that a psychically gifted child (or adult) could become open to spirit communication from angels, spirit guides, and even from spirits of anyone's loved ones, throughout the course of his or her day.

I add the reference to self-hypnosis as I completed a full course in hypnotherapy in December 2003 and became certified as a Certified Hypnotherapist or "CHT." Beyond what I was taught in that course, I have come to recognize that swinging is a wonderful way for any person to better access any messages or information from his or her inner self, the Universe, angels, and spirit guides. The simple rhythmic swaying of a swing really does help to bring a person—of any age—to a deeper level of relaxation. It is through complete relaxation that the conscious mind can "open up" to allow the spirit within to bring forth any messages that our Higher Power feels we need in any given moment.

As a child, and even as a tried-and-true adult, I have experienced many moments of strong intuitive insight that have come to me as I sat comfortably on a swing. I have also been made aware of spirit connections that happened in the relaxed, and generally happy, atmosphere of a child's playground. One such spirit connection comes to mind that I feel is important to share with my readers. That particular spirit connection involved my granddaughter Autumn, a young boy's spirit, a swing set, and myself, but first my readers need to understand the psychically gifted family tree that Autumn was born into.

∞

Psychic abilities are not something that happens genetically. There are families who do not have a single psychically gifted person among them, while other family trees seem to bear the fruit of many who are psychically gifted to some degree. As I have mentioned previously in this book, I am the only psychically gifted person among my immediate birth family members. My parents are not in possession of psychic abilities, nor are any of my four sisters psychically equipped in any way. In that way, I am alone. That said, every person among us has the gift of intuition within themselves, a statement that humankind will come to better understand, always in God's sense of perfect timing.

The Universe seems to have a reason for everything, and a sense of timing that I have learned is perfect in every way to achieve the maximum level of spiritual growth. That spirit growth is a constant throughout each of our respective lives. The fact that I was the only psychically gifted person within my immediate birth family did not mean that I would be left to fend for myself. I was always meant to know, and to share my life with, others who were also blessed with psychic abilities. I feel I was quite fortunate—and certainly blessed—to give birth to three sons, all healthy and strong in spirit. And as I would eventually learn, all were psychically gifted, but to varying degrees.

One of the biggest misconceptions about psychically gifted persons is that we all have the same abilities, and that we can all use those gifts to the same level. It is time to shed light on that myth. Each person who is born into a life with psychic abilities must choose to honor, and to respect, those gifts as our Higher Power guides him or her along the very unique path that is his or her life. If a psychically gifted person chooses to be negative, or disrespects the very gifts that God has blessed them with—or disrespects others who are gifted—then those gifts that allow them to connect in spirit will not stay open. In other words, psychic abilities cannot be used to promote negativity in the universe, or to bring harm to others. These gifts are wonderful and amazing tools that allow the Universe to bring spirit connections, messages, healing, and spiritual growth to humankind via people, like myself, who are psychically gifted. For example, just as those who are musically gifted can bring a sense of peace and understanding to our Earthly world through music, so, too, can the work and writings of positive, psychically gifted people.

The fact that I came into this world as the sole psychically gifted person in my birth family did not impede the strength of my gifts. That fact also did not alter the life path that I was meant to live. The additional fact that I gave birth to three sons—all psychically gifted—does not mean that I suddenly had psychic partners to bring into my business someday. Each of my three sons has had a very different life path thus far, although they have shared some of the same tough spiritual lessons such as addiction and abandonment, but in very unique ways.

My second son, Brady, committed suicide on December 31, 2000, without ever having had a discussion with me about his personal beliefs regarding his own psychic abilities. I can only recall one time that he "saw, heard, and felt" the energy of an old woman's spirit. That encounter took place at the home that his brother Brent's family lived in for a few years in the late 1990s. It is quite possible that Brady experienced other spirit connections during his lifetime, but that he never mentioned those to me. I believe that many of us have had spirit connections, but it takes something special to "open us up" so that we can better recognize the importance of these events.

It was through Brady's death that the Universe chose to "turn up the volume and intensity" on all of my psychic gifts. Even at that time of deep and painful grief, God made it clear to me that my life as a forty-six-year-old woman was never going to be the same. I will share more about that later, but I believe that Brady's life was one similar to other psychically gifted persons, in that he may have made use of his abilities in ways that were not as open, or as obviously psychic. Perhaps that is because the Universe does not yet require all of us to be operating at the kind of high level of psychic awareness that I live with everyday. I love my life, but there is no denying that it is certainly a daunting way of life. In that way, I find that our Higher

Power appears to be keeping life as psychically simple for humankind as possible, while allowing each person to grow into higher levels of spiritual awareness. As for Brady, I will never know if he might have brought his psychic abilities out and to the forefront of his life, had he lived longer. There is no doubt, in my mind, that his death was always meant to be the catalyst that would push me to use my gifts to help others.

∞

I have a third son, Blake, who is very strong in his psychic abilities, yet he has always appeared, to me, to be one who resists God's guidance to live openly as a psychically gifted individual. Blake's life path and spiritual lessons have taken him deep into a few addictions. In that way, my third son has not yet had many opportunities, as an adult, in which to truly help humankind with his gifts. However, when Blake was a child I often saw, felt, and heard his efforts to connect with others, always in very kind and compassionate ways. As a result, I have chosen to trust that God's plan for Blake will eventually allow his psychic gifts to be a powerful and positive compass for himself, and for all others. God certainly has provided me with enough proof to know that the life paths of each one of us are meant to affect all of humankind. We are all capable of doing great things, and in spite of any resistance that a person may have, our Higher Power always knows the ways by which each of us can be motivated to grow in spirit.

Blake has one son, a boy named Devin, whom the Universe has revealed, to me, is also a person whose spirit within is blessed with psychic abilities. The purpose for

Devin's gifts, and the ways in which he will be guided to use those gifts, has not yet been fully shown to me. As always, I continue to trust my intuitive guidance from the Universe and know that my grandson will be guided to use his gifts in positive ways, and in the sense of perfect timing that only God understands. In the meantime, I have chosen to be one of those persons, within my grandson's life, that he can count on to be an example of psychic and spiritual truth in action.

∞

My oldest son, Brent, is fairly open and accepting of his psychic gifts, but it is clear to both him and I that his path does not include working actively as a psychic medium. It appears to me that God's path for Brent is to use his psychic abilities and his strong intuition to make a visual impact through films. Films have long been a way for all of us to "face our fears," as well as to release feelings that may have been pent up for years. Some of those fears or emotions may even have been held in our spirits from past lives. Films have a way of opening us up to allow our spirits, minds, and bodies to connect in a way that we personally require to heal, to love, to find joy, and even to express anger in some healthy way.

Brent's films are all brought to his conscious awareness through the intuitive guidance that his spirit receives from our Higher Power, though he does not tend to think of his career in that way. Brent has been very supportive of my work as a psychic medium and author, just as I am of his life's work as a filmmaker. That said, Brent and I have very different ways by which God guides us to express ourselves through our words, actions, and deeds. Those very differences between us are what, I believe, allows us to do our best through his films and through my books.

Beyond the very differences that allow my eldest son and I to be the unique individuals that we are, I have also come to realize that he and I have a very close bond, one that has held us together through some of life's most trying times. Brent always seemed to be intuitive—to such a high level—that he seemed older and more mature than his peers. However, that sense of maturity and innate wisdom did not keep Brent from finding joy and laughter in his life. I was often guided by the Universe to notice how Brent could bring people together, and it was not uncommon for him to bring home "stray" children, in the way that some kids will bring home "stray puppies." Brent has always had the insight to recognize when another person needs to be included or accepted, although he does not suffer fools.

As my firstborn child, Brent was always expressing himself creatively. He loved to dress up and pretend he was a different character from whatever movie currently held his interest. Brent's love of artistic expression has been one of the common interests that has allowed the two of us to grow beyond the normal "mother and son relationship" to one in which we can respectfully discuss and encourage one another as creative peers.

Brent and I are both persistent and tenacious people, whose spirits within are willing to work tirelessly to achieve our life goals. We also have learned that we can both be rather stubborn, and in the ways that only the Universe can teach us, I believe that we have both begun to learn when it is the right time to "dig in our heels" and when it is best to "let it go." As a mother and son, I would say that Brent and I have come to a point within our relationship where we can love one another unconditionally—no matter our strengths or our weaknesses—while also staying true to the very individual beings that we are.

∞

Brent is the father of four daughters; three of them have already been revealed to me to be psychically gifted. Just as my three sons have always been very different in personality, and in the ways by which the Universe has guided them to make use of their psychic abilities, so, too, are these three granddaughters of mine. God has shown me visions, and given great detail on the life paths of each of my three psychic granddaughters, making it evident to me that not one of them is meant to follow in my direct footsteps.

I feel it is important to share this information with my readers. The ways by which each psychically gifted person is meant to impact the universe is varied and great. That said, there is no reason to judge one another or to disparage another's path in life. The work we do as psychically gifted beings is important, no matter how that work is expressed. No matter how young a person is when the Universe calls upon them to assist others, through psychic experiences and spirit connections, that person is capable of doing the job.

Brent's oldest daughter, Autumn, was quite young when her abilities to connect in spirit were revealed to her parents, and to me, as her grandmother. As the first grandchild brought into my life path, Autumn will always hold a special place in my heart, but it was the way she kept her heart open to others that impressed me most. This was a child, who was born into this life with a spirit full of special gifts, and she never felt the need to "hide them." Autumn did not tend to hold her gifts close, as so many psychically gifted people tend to.

From the time Autumn could speak it was obvious that she was never "alone." She played with her baby dolls and held tea parties for anyone who wanted to attend. By "anyone" I mean that this was a child who had no fear of sharing her playtime with angels, spirit guides, and occasionally, with the spirit of a child who had already died and crossed over to heaven.

Whenever I hear parents speak of their young son or daughter who has died, and they wonder if their child is okay in heaven, I think about the psychically gifted children, like Autumn, who are willing to stay wide open to spirit connections. In her own way, Autumn was a child who helped the Universe to bring healing and acceptance to the spirits of children who had lived very short lives. Kids are kids; they love to play and have little to no inhibitions about connecting in spirit.

Most children that I have met, who are psychically gifted, are not fearful until some adult tries to convince him or her that psychic abilities are "bad." How can loving others unconditionally be "bad?" How can doing the work of God and angels be "bad?" No, it is not psychic abilities that are "bad," but rather the fear that holds so many people locked in a cycle of perpetual judgement is where I perceive the negativity. I love psychically gifted children who, like Autumn, are willing to "be" perfect just as God created them.

Beyond the beautiful dolls, stuffed animals, and spirits made visible only to Autumn, that would keep her company as she played, my granddaughter was also visited by adult spirits. When this little girl was only three years old, the spirit of an old woman often visited her. Brent and his family were living in the old woman's home in Edina, Minnesota, as her adult son had moved her to a health care facility. Though the old woman had not yet died, her spirit would often soul travel back to her home where she discovered a little girl had the ability to sense her.

On many occasions my son and his wife would overhear conversations between Autumn and the old woman's spirit. Autumn's mother wasn't really fond of the visits, but she soon came to understand that the old woman was dying and that her spirit simply longed for more time in her home. My son Brent had no fear of his daughter's special gifts and did not attempt to dissuade her from using them. It was obvious to her parents that Autumn had no fear of the old woman's spirit and felt compassion towards her in the way that only a child can touch the heart of the elderly. Eventually the old woman died and her son sold the house, which forced Brent and his family to move to an apartment in a different city. To my knowledge, that ended the old woman's spirit visits to my granddaughter. The move did not deter Autumn's three-year-old self from communication with spirits. In fact, it was at the new apartment residence in Inver Grove Heights, Minnesota, that my psychic granddaughter made a young spirit friend named "Andy."

I was not personally made aware of Autumn's spirit friend, Andy, until late in the summer of 2002. By that time Autumn and her family had already moved to the basement apartment of our home in Shakopee, Minnesota. Conversations of psychic encounters with spirits had become a normal way of life for us. Living as three generations within one large home allowed for the Universe to guide each one of us to develop our gifts to our personal highest and best level. Keep in mind that psychic abilities do not stay stagnant; each person's gifts can be strengthened by use and will always be open to whatever degree our Higher Power allows.

∞

My own psychic gifts had been opened wide since my son Brady's death, and in every way possible, God, angels, and spirit guides had been guiding me to keep developing my psychic senses. Occasionally, the spirit of a departed loved one was brought through, by God, to connect with me in some psychic way.

At the same time, I was working hard to heal from the deep grief caused by the suicide death of a son that I truly loved and missed. In spite of my grief, it was apparent to me that the Universe clearly felt that I could best heal by helping others. Through my strong intuition I found that my Higher Power made all things known to me. It was apparent to me that the amazing psychic gifts that God had given to my spirit, were available for me to use as fully and completely as possible in my life path. As I have mentioned previously in my book, I have use of all five of the psychic senses—sight, sound, smell, taste, and the ability to feel spirits, and all energy, in a multitude of ways. I will be helping my readers to understand psychic abilities to as deep of a level as possible, in the ways I am guided intuitively to share them, through my writing and my work.

The psychic gifts I have within me allow me to see spirits in many ways, including, but not limited to: orbs, mist and shadow forms, partial and full hologram images, fluid images, and even in a form that allows me to see spirits that appear to be as solid in mass as any living physical body. My psychic gift of sight allows me to "see" spirits both in my third eye region of my spirit, or "the mind's eye" as it is sometimes called, as well as I can "see" spirits with my physical eyes. The way I can "see" spirits is not in my control, but rather I have come to understand that it is the Universe who determines the best and highest way for any spirits to share communication at any given time.

The fact that my granddaughter Autumn has her own level of psychic abilities is important to my story, but one must remember that we are two people whose spirits are at different levels of spiritual and psychic growth. In that way, the Universe has asked me, on many occasions, to assist my granddaughter in better understanding her own psychic abilities. In addition, I am not to interfere with her personal life path, or the ways in which she feels is best to utilize her psychic gifts—or even to *not* use them—at any given time. As a grandmother, and as a psychic mentor to Autumn, that could create rather a conundrum if I were to ignore my strong intuitive guidance from God. I realized many years ago that I had to not only accept *my* life path, but that it is also best if I accept God's paths for all others, whether those people are my family, my close friends, or even total strangers. We all must travel through our lives in the ways that our Higher Power deems is best for our personal spiritual growth.

During those first few years after Brady's death, it felt to me as though my own psychic education was moving so fast that it did not allow time for me to feel afraid of my gifts, nor to fear the awesome responsibilities that came with them. I was learning fast that I had to be ready for anything—and at any time. Our Higher Power seemed intent on placing people and spirits into such close proximity to my life path that I could not ignore them.

In spite of all the busy energy that filled my life, I found myself guided to spend time with my grandchildren on a fairly regular basis. As the first and oldest grandchild, I found Autumn to be delightful company on those days when I felt the urge for a walk-and-talk outdoors with a child. As a young child, Autumn was very insightful; she appeared to have a deeper grasp on the world than most young children that I have previously known. Autumn's vocabulary was extensive for a child, which created the opportunity for interesting dialogue between us.

After one such walk together we found ourselves at the playground of the park that was located directly across the street from our home. The weather was cooperative in a way that made us feel as though we did not yet want to return to our respective living spaces within the large home that Bob and I owned. Autumn wanted to play on the swing set and I, too, felt that the two of us needed to linger outdoors a while longer. I urged Autumn to "Climb up on a swing" so that I could give her a push. Autumn was six-and-one-half years old at that time, and capable of swinging herself, but she welcomed my offer to get her started with a big push.

I could feel that my inner child wanted to join Autumn on the swings that day. That said, my responsible adult self knew that I could not join her on the empty swing, located just to her left. Back surgery just three years prior had created a situation in which it was no longer comfortable for me to sit on the type of "U" shaped swings that our neighborhood playground was equipped with. Instead of swinging, I found a comfortable perch on a nearby picnic table, and relaxed as I watched my granddaughter enjoy her time on the swingset.

The playground was empty on that beautiful summer day, save for Autumn and myself, so I was curious when I noticed Autumn talking aloud to someone. There were two of the "U" shaped swings on that particular swing set plus a large, padded, red swing that parents could use to gently swing a baby or toddler. As I continued to observe my young granddaughter I noticed that she kept turning her head to speak to the empty "U" shaped swing located on her left. Autumn seemed quite intent on her conversation, even as she continued all of the physical movements required to keep a swing in constant motion. I stood up and quietly made my way closer to the swing set as I was more than curious about with "whom" she might be conversing. The closer I moved to the swing set, the more I could hear her saying. By moving closer I felt that I could also easily see every part of what was transpiring.

It was apparent to me that Autumn was communicating with the spirit of a young child simply because of the nature of her conversation. However, I did not want to assume anything. Eventually I felt it was time to interrupt her youthful chatter and to gain clarity about the situation. Just as I opened my mouth to speak, Autumn turned her attention to me and asked if I would like to meet her friend, Andy. I replied, "Sure, where is he?" as he was still not being revealed to me through my psychic abilities, yet it was clear to me that Autumn could see and hear him. Autumn held tight to the chains on her swing as she pointed with one of the fingers on her left hand and said, "He's right there, Grandma; he's on the other swing!"

As hard as I tried I was not able to "see" the young boy's spirit nor could I "hear" him speak at that time. My intuition, those gut instincts that we all have, gave me the sense that it was very important for Autumn to have this opportunity to communicate with little Andy's spirit and that I was to assist in whatever ways that the Universe needed of me. All of that was important, regardless of the fact that only Autumn was given the opportunities to see and to hear Andy's spirit at that time.

I stood nearby watching, and listening to Autumn's side of the conversation, when my attention suddenly shifted to the empty swing to her left. The swing began moving—forwards and backwards—in the same way it would if a living child in a physical body had been seated there, pumping his or her legs, and shifting his or her upper body to gain momentum. I smiled as Autumn continued to talk to her spirit friend, and to cheer him on, as he, too, was swinging all on his own! I felt exhilarated to be able to share in this psychic event with my granddaughter.

Soon Autumn began sharing some of the conversation that had taken place with her young spirit friend, telling me that they had met previously when her family lived in an apartment in Inver Grove Heights, Minnesota. Autumn had lived there with her family for approximately seven months, and had met Andy's spirit just as she had turned four years old. She explained to me that he had visited her often during those months, but she had not "seen" him since she had moved to Shakopee to live in our basement apartment.

My granddaughter seemed happy to receive this visit from her spirit friend, as she had been concerned about him. As I listened to all that Autumn had to say I realized that the little boy's spirit was "stuck" on the Earthly plane of existence and that God had brought him to Autumn so that he could be helped.

About ten minutes into the conversation with Autumn I began to notice that Andy's spirit was making himself psychically visible to me in my third eye, or the mind's eye as it is often called. I "saw" Andy as a cute little boy with sandy blond hair and a few freckles. It appeared to me that he was about five or six years old, and he liked to wear pajamas with cowboys and Indians printed on the fabric. I had the strong sense that he was beginning to trust me simply by virtue of the fact that my granddaughter was unafraid to talk to me about him.

There was a strong psychic feeling that his spirit emitted that told me he really felt bad about his death. I was allowed to feel that his mother was still deep in grief, and that he felt, somehow, responsible for making his mommy cry so much. In an instant God revealed a vision—almost like a movie within my spirit's mind—that allowed me to "see" this little boy's death.

I was psychically shown that his death had occurred shortly before his sixth birthday, when he was outdoors happily playing with a large, red ball. As so many children tend to do, God showed me that Andy had become so engrossed in his play that he forgot to watch for cars when his ball rolled into the road. I was shown that a moving vehicle had hit the little boy instantly.

Next an angel told, and showed me, psychically, that this little boy had been taken by ambulance to a hospital, where he died a few days later. The boy's mother had been overwhelmed with guilt, and had plunged deep into a depression that had lasted many years already. In spite of the efforts of many angels, spirit guides, and the spirits of loved ones, young Andy's spirit had remained "stuck" here in the Earthly level of existence. He had been trying hard to comfort his mother, albeit in spirit form. Unfortunately, young Andy's spirit had great difficulty in communicating with his mother. She was too blocked with the negative energy and pain of grief that had been brought on by the loss of her son.

As all of this was revealed to me, I felt such a strong desire to help the Universe by assisting that little boy's spirit. Andy's spirit needed to get to the Light. I understood that Andy's willingness to connect with Autumn, and now with me, was key to his crossing over. I also felt that we would have to be patient with young Andy as he was still not quite ready to take that step on his own. I knew that God would guide my granddaughter, young Andy's spirit, and me, when it was the perfect time for his crossing.

When it was time to leave the park Autumn said her goodbyes to her spirit friend, and then turned to point in the direction of our home. She said it was important for Andy's spirit to know where she lived. To my delight, Andy's spirit said, "Goodbye, Autumn's grandma!" and gave me a big smile as he hopped off of his swing. I paused to watch as the swing slowed to a complete stop. I then took Autumn's hand in mine as we walked the short distance to our home, each deep in our own thoughts, unsure as to when the Universe would bring Andy's spirit through to connect with us again. I could not explain to my granddaughter that my intuitive senses were allowing me to feel that this encounter with a little boy's spirit would have a great impact on the two of us. My work as a psychic medium has taught me that the Universe maximizes all opportunities so that each of us can learn and grow in spiritual knowledge, through all things. And while "swinging" may appear to be simple child's play, I knew that God's hand was hard at work in connecting Autumn and me, with her old friend, Andy, on that day.

∞

Autumn did not have to wait long to visit with her spirit friend, Andy, as she began to notice him spending a lot of time in her room, always playing with her toys. He seemed fascinated by some of her more "modern" toys. It was clear to me that this little boy's spirit had been "stuck" in a sense of spiritual limbo for a long time. He reminded me of a young boy who would have grown up in the late 1940s or perhaps in the early 1950s. That said, I was also aware that the years in which Andy had lived were not really important. Autumn and I did not need to know that information in order to help that young boy's spirit.

Over a period of two weeks Autumn got so many visits from Andy's spirit that she began to grow tired from lack of sleep. She brought this to my attention when I was visiting with her one afternoon as she kept yawning while we talked. I asked her why she was so tired and she mentioned that Andy's spirit had been waking her up for several nights in a row. He wanted Autumn to play with him with some of her "really fun toys."

I smiled as I recalled how many nights visiting spirits have disturbed my sleep. That is one of the downsides of being psychically gifted, as spirits tend to forget that a psychically gifted person is still living a life and has a mind and physical body that need rest.

As I looked at my exhausted granddaughter I knew that the time had come for young Andy's spirit to be assisted. It was time for him to cross over to heaven so that he could be with God, angels, and his departed loved ones. I had already learned much through the death experience of my own son, Brady. I have come to realize that every spirit needs to cross over to the healing plane of existence. Again this is a space of energy that I refer to as "heaven" or "the other side."

Crossing over to heaven allows each spirit the opportunities to make full use of the healing that our Higher Power affords us. In as much as little Andy's spirit wanted to help his mother in her grief, I felt the urging from God and angels to help him return to his true home, with God. In that way, both Andy's spirit and his mother could truly begin to heal within, as her son would not be stuck in the energy between death and the after-life.

∞

That evening I sat quietly in my favorite, old rocking chair as I tuned-in with God and angels. Without delay, the answers to my unspoken questions about Andy's spirit, came clearly to my conscious mind: I was to assist God by communicating with the little boy's spirit, angels, and even the spirit of Andy's now-deceased grandmother. In short, I was to perform a spirit crossing to aid a spirit who was stuck after death in a place that he would no longer be allowed to haunt. In as much as my granddaughter Autumn and her spirit friend could relate well to one another, it was important for each of us to keep moving forward in our lives. Equally important was the fact that Andy's spirit needed to be with God, so that he could choose to heal.

Through my work as a psychic medium I have been guided to assist the Universe with spirit crossings many times, but I soon learned that *this time* would be very different. To my surprise, God and angels made it absolutely clear to me that my six-year-old granddaughter was to assist me in helping her spirit friend to complete his crossing. As the information came to me I questioned whether or not Autumn was ready for that kind of psychic work, simply because of her Earthly age. The answer came swiftly, and rang true to my inner self: *The Universe, God, our Higher Power, our Creator, always knows what each of us can truly handle and never gives us more than we are ready for, no matter what name we assign to that Being of energy that unites and guides all of us.*

I felt calm and at peace as I reached for the telephone, knowing that I must explain the situation to my son Brent. It was not enough for me, alone, to understand the importance of Autumn's participation in the spirit crossing exercise. My son and his wife also had to be accepting of God's guidance for their daughter.

Within a few minutes I hung up the phone as Brent and I had concluded our discussion. Seconds later, Autumn knocked on my kitchen door as her parents had sent her upstairs to join me in the living room of our modest home. The two of us sat down and made ourselves comfortable as I explained to Autumn the nature of God's guidance to me. Autumn listened intently as I described "how" she could help Andy's spirit to join God, angels, and even her uncle Brady, in heaven.

Maybe it was the fact that Autumn has never had to hide her psychic gifts within her immediate birth family, or maybe it was because she and I had prior discussions about God, angels, life, and even death, that she seemed completely at ease. She was eager to help her spirit friend. Autumn reminded me of how sad Andy's spirit felt to her, even though he loved the fact that he had found a young friend, like Autumn, who could "see, hear, and feel" the energy of his spirit.

No spirit can truly be happy when they are stuck in a state of limbo, no matter what the circumstances were that first held him or her back from crossing over immediately after his or her Earthly death. Young Andy's spirit was no exception. Fortunately, neither Autumn, nor myself, had to wait for the little boy's spirit to connect psychically with us; he seemed quite ready and willing to join his grandmother's spirit as she appeared at his side in my living room.

I explained to Autumn, and also to Andy's spirit, just how important it is for our spirits within to rejoin our Higher Power, whom I call God, after our physical bodies die on Earth. People die from many different causes and at all different ages, and in all cases, it is important for the spirit within to go home to heaven for healing.

The child still in a physical body, and the spirit child, both listened intently as I explained that Andy needed to trust God and angels to care for his mother. I explained that while she was still in a prolonged state of grief, God and angels would take care of his mother, just as they were helping me to heal from the grief of my son's death.

At that moment we were joined in the living room by Brady's spirit. His visit spurred me to further explain to the children that God *does* allow angels, spirit guides, and even the spirits of our loved ones, to visit us occasionally, but they cannot stay here all of the time. Brady's spirit helped Andy to understand that heaven is a wonderful place of healing energy, and just like Brady, young Andy's spirit would never be alone.

Love, healing energy, and a sense of peace sprang forth from Brady's spirit so that Andy's spirit could feel what awaited him on the other side of the veil. I "saw" Andy smile as he felt all of that amazing energy. At that exact moment, a brilliant white light revealed itself to my right, and to Autumn's left, in the area where my living room joins the dining room. The white light was so bright that it blocked out the images of my dining room chairs and table that were somewhere "beyond" that white light. My own psychic abilities were open wide making everything clear and obvious to me. I wondered what Autumn was being allowed to view or to feel in those moments, so I asked her to describe anything that she noticed.

Autumn had a big smile on her face and was waving at Andy's spirit as he stepped "into the Light." She described it as "Andy walking into God." I felt that Autumn was exceptionally astute as she described the same sense of white light imagery that I had been seeing. Both of us had observed two angels that had appeared at the edge of the Light, and who stood, one on each side of "the Light."

When the Light had appeared, my granddaughter and I both saw that the spirit of Andy's grandmother was no longer in our living room. It appeared to us that she was now further back in the Light, as if she had walked deeper into a tunnel filled with the Light. It all felt wonderful to me, and Autumn seemed overjoyed for her spirit friend.

I urged Andy to "Go into the Light" and felt so much emotion fill my heart as he smiled and waved goodbye to me, too. Andy seemed to be almost giddy with happiness. He held out his hands, to accept a helping hand from each of the angels, as he went skipping into the tunnel of Light. The last thing I saw was his grandmother's spirit, smiling, as the angels and Andy's spirit disappeared into the Light.

Just as suddenly as the spirit crossing began—it was over. My granddaughter and I were filled with an overwhelming sense of love and joy in our hearts. As I reached for a tissue to dry my eyes, I was suddenly aware of a wonderful "hugging" energy that I was feeling from my son Brady's spirit, as his visit, too, was over. I could no longer hold back the tears. These spirit visits and spirit crossings can bring those of us who are psychically gifted, to a level of spiritual joy that it is almost indescribable.

As for Autumn, well, I could not have been prouder of her! I know that God had fostered her relationship with young Andy's spirit. Even as a young child herself, my granddaughter had been accepting of all that the spirit connection with Andy was meant to bring into her life.

Autumn did not act selfishly when it was time for her friend to go home to heal. In the weeks and months that followed, both Autumn and I were blessed to receive a couple of spirit visits from Andy. Those visits were only to say, "Thank you!" and to let us know how well he was doing back home in heaven.

My granddaughter is now seventeen years old, but her memories of young Andy's spirit are as vivid as mine and bring an instant smile to both of our faces. Autumn and I are pretty sure that Andy's spirit is still just-a-swingin' on some playground in heaven—and that when he does—he remembers his Earthly playmate Autumn, and her Grandma Robin!

CHAPTER THREE

Politics As Usual

There is an old phrase that is often bandied about in the media during the course of any year that is ripe with major political elections. I never thought much about that phrase until the Universe gave me two up-close and personal views of politics that I will never forget. The phrase I am referring to is "politics as usual." At first glance, I am fairly certain my readers will not assign much thought or emotion to those words as we have all been bombarded by political influences during election campaigns. Political ads, and political debates, seem to overwhelm us as they flood all of the media sources within range of our eyes and our ears. How surprised we are, at times, to find politicians knocking on the front doors of our homes—smiling and offering to shake our hands—in an effort to gain support, or to sway our votes in his or her favor. While all of that political campaigning might cause any one of us to feel overwhelmed, or even to feel jaded about our political choices, we should never forget that the Universe has brought countless people to live in the United States of America as a way to learn and to grow in spirit.

"Politics as usual" has long been a way of life in the country I was born, raised, and where I continue to reside. A country that, I believe, is made whole by the uniquely individual beings we are, and who call this place "home."

My psychic sense is that the Universe began a spiritual process to forge a bond between people of all nationalities, races, cultures, and religions, by intuitively guiding those people/spirits to a mass of land on Earth that we refer to as the United States of America. The sense I get, from God, is that the concept of bringing humankind together, in this way, began long before I was born in 1954, and will continue long after I have completed my life journey. The very notion that people, with so many differences, can learn to recognize that they are all very much alike, seems— at least on the surface—to be something that babies and young children have always known. That begs the questions: Why is it that so many people tend to grow up and forget what is really important? What are the *real* insights that our Higher Power is trying to convey to all who reside in the United States of America? And how does what we learn affect, not only the rest of the Earthly world, but how does it affect the entire universe? The only way I can begin to answer those questions—and any of the questions that will follow—is to share with my readers some of what I have learned through the intuitive guidance that I have received from the Universe thus far. Bear in mind that politics will always be another tool for our Higher Power to bring us to greater levels of spiritual growth, no matter what political persuasion any of us are drawn to during our lives.

∞

One thing I know, for certain, is that we have a long and arduous history in this country of trying to right the wrongs that have befallen our families, friends, and neighbors. For the most part, I feel—deep within my spirit's heart—that the majority of people try to create political and social change from a place of positive intention.

My observations have allowed me to know that the greatest motivating factors for political change are always seeded in personal strife. Whenever a person has been personally affected—by any life occurrence that caused them to believe that "politics as usual" was lacking in some way—he or she will not rest until they become a part of the political process for change. The reason a person cannot rest, in those circumstances, is because his or her spirit within has been touched by the energy of injustice. And until that person's spirit makes personal efforts to change the political system, that person will not be able to view life in any other way.

It is important to remember that "how" any person perceives injustice, as well as "how" that person believes humankind can benefit by political changes, is always influenced by his or her personal life experiences. Only the passage of time, and humankind's reflection on history, can provide an accurate measure of the value of any politician's contributions.

The majority of men or women, who have found themselves deeply immersed in the energy and action of political change, are not in it for the money, nor for any sense of "fame." These men and women also do not perceive a life working in politics, as an easy way to live their life paths.

As a general rule of thumb, working for political change brings a person under so much personal scrutiny that he or she must learn quickly to surround him or herself with firm, healthy, and positive boundaries. To serve humankind, in the political arena, requires a person to open up wide—in the intuitive sense—as that is the only way to truly measure the *real* needs of the people.

The job of "politician" also requires a person to tap into the larger energy of the entire universe, as the issues that humankind faces today are not new. Sadly, the issues that all of humankind is dealing with in 2013 are the same things that have always plagued us. There have always been wars, famine, disease, murders, rape, and a great imbalance of power and wealth between various peoples. No matter what period of time we review in the history of humankind, we will always find the same cycle of issues affecting us. Perhaps it is time to look closer at the issues that our Higher Power has placed within our life paths, and to view them through a more spiritual lens. My intuition has guided me—many times, and through many different situations—to step back and to view everything from "the bigger picture" lens of spirituality that only the Universe can provide. By viewing all things, including, but not limited to politics, through the broader lens of spiritual growth, I have come to truly know about, and to understand, many things.

∞

I know that most people do not want to see their families, friends, or neighbors go hungry, lose their homes or jobs, or suffer through painful or debilitating illnesses. Most people do not really care what color another person's skin is, or how a person chooses to connect in private prayer to our Higher Power. Most people do not really care which candidate their family members, friends, neighbors, and coworkers voted for, because the final results will always be brought to our awareness through mass media. For the most part, this political process allows each of us to maintain a shroud of privacy, regarding our political choices, during any election.

Most people do not really care about the birthplace of origin of their friends, neighbors, and coworkers, but they do want to experience the ease of clear communication. The common denominator that truly allows each of us to get past our differences in life, and to find common ground, is the ability to communicate clearly and effectively. None of us want to feel as though our individual needs are ignored. That said, the only way to ensure our voices are heard is to find a way to communicate as effectively as possible.

In the arena of politics, the ability to communicate well is of paramount importance. A political leader, whose voice and votes do not reflect the needs of his or her constituents, will always find that the Universe seems to pull the proverbial political rug out from under his or her feet. Another person, one who will, hopefully, foster clear and concise communication, soon replaces them. Through those efforts, positive results will be experienced throughout the entire world.

Clear and concise communication—that certainly doesn't appear to be too difficult, does it? That sounds like an easy solution to a problem that has revealed itself in chaos, wars, economic depressions, and in the complete obliteration of entire societies, since time began. A problem that often reveals itself in such things as religious judgment, bigotry, and political discord. A problem that, I believe, is rooted in the innate spiritual need we all have within us to be unconditionally loved—exactly as we are—in any given moment.

We all want to believe that *we* are unconditionally lovable; yet, we often view the world through a very narrow lens. That narrow lens does not allow us to comprehend that if *we* are loveable, exactly as *we are*, then how can all of the other people in the world—*who are different from us*—also be worthy of unconditional love? That narrow lens has long extended itself to every field of expertise, including, but not limited to, politics. Political foes have long focused our attention on what is "wrong" with his or her political opponent—and what is "wrong" with the rest of the world—rather than focusing on all of the ways by which humankind is alike.

In the 1800s this narrow lens that I speak of nearly destroyed the United States of America when civil war broke out, and neighbors found themselves fighting against neighbors. Entire families and towns were torn apart by political principles. Lines were drawn on maps that forever changed the way the people in this country viewed one another.

Humankind became entrenched in a series of battles that focused—as most wars do—*on changing the viewpoints of others*. Through the might and the force of soldiers—armed not only with weapons meant to kill—but also armed with orders from the leading politicians of that time, human beings chose to kill one another.

Changes that were meant to free men, women, and children of color were not brought about by any positive, thoughtful, or respectful means that would allow all involved to come to his or her own place of understanding, but through the ugly actions and energy of war.

My psychic sense is that humankind is often too impatient to trust in God's sense of perfect timing. As a result, the choice is frequently made by politicians to act against that which appalls us, or confuses us, by engaging the might of any country's military forces. Of course, no politician acts alone. There are always people who choose to join ranks, for any cause that stirs us, deep within our spirits' hearts. But as I was guided to write this chapter about politics, I was also made fully aware of how foolish the trend is for humankind to keep killing one another in the name of war. The energy that the Universe, whom I call God, allows me to feel is the futility of human beings fighting one another over our differences. Rather than to keep working at strengthening our connections as spirits by recognizing our commonalities, and by applauding each other's strengths, we keep choosing to kill one another.

I have never considered myself to be politically motivated, and to that I could add that I am not one who is easily swayed by political fervor or rhetoric. I am certainly not persuaded by the violence or destruction of wars. That said, there *are* times when I have found that God has been able to get my attention, and to hold it with regards to politics, and those whose lives have been devoted to serving others within that Earthly political arena.

Two such times come to mind, that I have now been guided to share with my readers. These two examples that I am about to share, are not only amazing spirit encounters, but I believe these were two spirits whose lives were lived, in such a way, as to forever leave a mostly positive imprint on their personal pieces of political history. I say "mostly" positive because each of the politician's spirits that I connected with had lives that were filled with long and difficult spiritual lessons. In that way, each of them would have experienced the good, the bad, and the ugly, that life seems to share with us all. And, as I discovered, each of these former politicians had good insights to share from the Other Side.

∞

One day, in the winter of 2003, I found myself painting watercolors alongside my granddaughter, Autumn. At that time, Autumn—the oldest grandchild in our family—had already revealed her love of watercolor painting, as well as the fact that she was psychically gifted. Her parents had felt guided, through their personal sense intuition, to home school their very bright and gifted child. In that way, they felt she would be allowed to learn, and to grow, in the ways that were best for her life path.

On that cold winter day in 2003, Autumn had already completed her home schooling studies for the day. Her parents had allowed her to join me, upstairs, for an impromptu art session. I always looked forward to those occasional opportunities when the two of us could share time as grandmother and granddaughter. I also felt it was important that I continue to instruct Autumn in the art of watercolor painting, something I had been passionate about since I was a teenager. In Autumn I also recognized a kindred "artist" spirit, one who seemed to have a special talent for drawing and painting.

Autumn and I sat together at an old, six-foot long table that I had claimed, long ago, as the place in my home where I could set up my art supplies to paint or draw. That old table provided a place where I could allow my imagination to flow through the creative part of my spirit within. The date was February 17, 2003, which had been designated a national holiday in the United States, one commonly referred to as President's Day. To celebrate the significance of the day, my granddaughter and I had decided that we would each paint something to honor one of the past presidents of our country. President Abraham Lincoln soon became our agreed upon choice, to commemorate through our artistic endeavors that day. We each began sketching out whatever painting idea had come to mind. As we began to create art, I quizzed my nearly seven-year-old granddaughter on what she had already learned about Abraham Lincoln, one of our most famous past presidents.

Autumn had recently learned a few facts about the 16th president of the United States of America, one of which was the fact that he had been the president in office when slavery was abolished. She also knew that he was the president who had issued the Emancipation Proclamation, though she was unclear as to what those two words meant.

At the age of seven Autumn really could not comprehend the importance of President Lincoln's role in our country, nor what slavery truly meant. She needed a tangible way to relate to President Abraham Lincoln. We discussed the fact that Lincoln's portrait has been imprinted on one side of every single U.S. penny that Autumn or myself had ever seen, as well as he is also featured on the U.S. five dollar bill.

My granddaughter also knew the timeless story that Abraham Lincoln had grown up in a log cabin, yet he had been given the opportunities in his life path to become a famous politician in our country. Soon our discussion dwindled as our thoughts centered more on the artistic process that we were each involved in that day. All was quiet within the sanctuary of my home office when the Universe brought forth the spirit of a famous, yet humble man . . . President Abraham Lincoln.

On that particular day it was me who first became aware of the spirit that had entered my home. I noticed the spirit of a man, who stood just to the right of the table that held the artwork, that Autumn, and I, had begun just moments earlier. I "saw" the spirit of Abraham Lincoln as God allowed him to show himself to me through the third eye portion of my psychic sight.

To my surprise, the spirit of our former sixteenth president did not present an image of pomp and circumstance, instead I "saw" him dressed in older, worn clothing. He did not have a beard, but he did look old, even in spirit.

I soon noticed that he was standing, (in spirit,) within a farmer's field. He seemed to be urging me to take note of the fact that he was "at home" as I saw him. By that I mean that he was conveying the sense, to me, that the *real* spirit of the man (previously known as President Abraham Lincoln) was far more content to be working hard in a farmer's field than to be creating the illusion that he, somehow, knew anything about politics. Mind you, that was *his* message as we talked in the spirit language of energy. The message he conveyed is not a reflection of any personal views that I might have about his political legacy.

Since the mid-1800s, when Abraham Lincoln was knee-deep in political strife as a leader of men, women, and children, in the United States of America, most of us have been taught, but a mere page in the life of a man, who certainly made his mark on history. Only the scholars who have been guided to study the life of the man called Abraham Lincoln could have possibly come close to knowing the true heart of such a complicated man.

It is my belief that most of humankind has come to know the man, Abraham Lincoln, as only an illusion that was created by the complexity of the times in which he lived. A man whose spirit within was now standing in my home office, conveying to me that he would have been more than content if God had allowed him to live life as a simple, hardworking, farmer of the land.

Lincoln's spirit told me that he understands the land, as the soil is something that gives back to a person, generally in direct proportion to the efforts and energy that one gives to it. The land is there before we are born, and will be there long after we die, as it helps God to perpetuate life. Soil, seeds, compost, and a gentle rain, are what fed the spirit of the man we came to know as Abraham Lincoln.

His spirit told me that he does not want to be referenced as "President Lincoln" any longer. The heaviness, that still resides within his spirit's energy from that life, cannot be ignored. That was a hard life, indeed, for his spirit to have experienced. My intuitive sense is that he will remain on the Other Side, in heaven, for a good, long while. He has chosen to work on healing his spirit with assistance from God and angels.

"Mr. Lincoln," I say, but he quickly rejects the title and asks that I call him "Abraham." I feel his sadness, but stronger yet, is the energy of humility that comes from his spirit towards mine. No matter that our society has long revered him for his efforts to abolish slavery. No matter that he was the man God asked to lead the United States of America during the challenging times of the civil war. This is a spirit who remains disheartened by the life that his Higher Power had guided him to live through, way back in the 1800s. One cannot escape the imprint that life has left upon the spirit of Abraham Lincoln.

I feel the need to ask him about what I am feeling and his reply still echoes deep within me. His spirit tells me, "I am sickened by the fact that mankind could not come to understand that slavery is wrong without having to be legislated toward its conclusion. I am further disappointed by the fact that mankind . . . human beings of all races . . . continue to disrespect one another. This is why I focus my energy upon, and look for my healing from, the land." Powerful words, indeed, from a spirit who rejects the notion that he was a powerful man in the life he lived as President Abraham Lincoln.

With a quiet nod of his spirit's head, and the faintest of smiles, the spirit of one of the most influential past presidents of the United States of America disappeared from my view, and from all of my psychic senses. I heard myself emit a heavy sigh, as if my own spirit within had to release the negative energy that my visitor had brought with him.

I turned to ask Autumn if she had also seen our visiting spirit. My granddaughter nodded her head "yes," but kept working on the painting she had begun. Her painting featured President Abraham Lincoln in his famous stovepipe hat pose—which happened to be the way Lincoln's spirit revealed himself to *her*!

Autumn never saw Lincoln the way I did, nor did she hear all of the things that his spirit conveyed to me, during the spirit connection in February 2003. Why? It is because she did not need to. The Universe did not allow my young granddaughter to feel the sadness, the humility, nor the heaviness of the spirit known as President Abraham Lincoln. In this case, the Universe felt she was too young, and that she would not have understood the significance of those messages within the spirit's visit. I am grateful that God gave me the opportunity to experience, and to write about, yet another powerfully moving spirit connection. I will continue to pray for Abraham's spirit to heal.

∞

As amazing as that spirit connection was to experience, and to share with my readers, the Universe is clearly intent on pushing me to *"Write more!"* in this very socially conscious chapter. My mind now wanders to recall some of the great inventions and discoveries that have come from the minds of people who were born, and raised, in nearly every corner of the globe. Inventions and discoveries that have allowed humankind to continue to grow, and to flourish, in spite of the Earthly challenges that the Universe places in each of our paths. Inventions and discoveries that may have even taken root as far back as Abraham Lincoln's time on Earth.

People who spoke different languages than you or I, lived under different political regimes, and ate different foods, have all participated in these inventions and discoveries. Many of those people found a specific religious or spiritual path by which to connect with a higher power, whose name varies within every single religious path. I would venture to add that some of those people—whose minds brought forth great changes for humankind—might not have ever found their personal, spiritual connection to the Universe. Instead, he or she may have found the greatest solace within the work provided by his or her niche of expertise.

Additionally, some of the greatest thinking minds—in all fields, including politics—have not come to us via traditional educational methods. Rather, they have been men and women who have felt compelled to follow the intuitive guidance that came from a place deep within him or her. And I dare say, each of them followed that intuitive guidance, until they completed the personal missions of his or her life path. My sense is that the journey of their lives was equally as important as whatever discovery or bit of great knowledge that their personal work brought to humankind. Simply put, every moment of the journeys of our life paths are every bit as important as what we have achieved when we reach our final destinations.

From the minds of seemingly ordinary men, and women, have come many new discoveries. Even since my birth in 1954, the discoveries have continued, often forcing humankind to accept technological advancements profound enough to stagger the mind. And yet, we are never done growing or learning.

The great minds of our time have produced amazing tools by which we can connect with, and communicate with, others around the globe, and in a sense of timing that is nearly instantaneous. As our ability to reach others has expanded, I find that it has become more important than ever, for all of us to find the easiest way possible, to communicate clearly. In addition, our personal political views must be tempered with a sense of "what we can live with" in our specific country of origin, but we cannot stop there. We must also include a positive sense of energy towards "what others can live with," too, as the tools of global communication bring us closer to one another in spirit, mind, and body.

All of these thoughts bring me back to the phrase "politics as usual." I realize that those three words can translate to completely different perceptions of how each of us views the role of politics within our town, our state, our country, and throughout the world. "Politics as usual" is *not* the answer to positive communication and healthy relations between all people. Why? Because "politics as usual" suggests that no changes are needed. One look at any news station, or any newspaper—in any country, on any given day—will reveal the truth of the current Earthly political structure: *It is not working*! And my life has taught me well, that if something isn't working, then it needs to be examined closely.

At times I can see that a few repairs or changes are all that is needed, but in most cases, I find that the Universe, whom I call God, guides me to "take a step back in my spirit shoes" so that I can gain a new perspective on any problem. It is only through my own willingness to "step back," and to view a problem through the wide-open lens of positive, spiritual enlightenment and growth, that I am able to move forward in the energy of change.

Change is never easy, and the task that lies before humankind is, indeed, a daunting one. That said, I know the answer to better communication lies in the innate ability that each of us possesses to live intuitively. In simple terms, we are all made up of spirit, mind, and body, with a direct connection to our Higher Power, and to one another, through the energy of the universe. It is within that vast, never-ending, flow of energy that our intuition links us to one another, and forever to our Higher Power.

The answers that will guide humankind to a more positive political agenda for the world have already begun to flow through the intuition of many people. Some of the people that I speak of have been, or will be, voted into a place of political power by his or her constituents. Others have risen to, or will rise to, a throne of power through the birth process, as his or her country's parliament has proclaimed. Still others are in the process to recover, or to reclaim, their beloved homeland, from years of harsh rule by dictators.

In all cases, I believe that the Universe has been pushing, prodding, and guiding humankind intuitively towards a new political horizon. I "see" this new political horizon does not exclusively serve one small segment of the Earth's population. Instead, it will reveal a sense of political connection that will unite humankind forever. And through the action, reaction, and interaction, of each person/spirit, we will be able to feel the energy of all that is positive as we strive for a world that is balanced in its best and highest form.

∞

As I write this chapter I find that the Universe has opened up a window, so to speak, to allow me to view politics on the Earthly plane of existence. Within this "window" is a place where I am kept safe from all of the turmoil and confusion that encompasses the world at this time. The Earthly calendar lists today's date as January 6, 2012, but that does not appear to really be important. The spiritual lessons of social harmony that humankind has been guided through have gone on since the beginning of our existence. The intuitive guidance that I have received to incorporate today's date, feels as though it is meant to be placed on a timeline of social and political change, one that will lead us all to a place of peaceful coexistence. That sense, deep within my psychically gifted inner self, is immediately followed by the awareness that the level of social and political peace and harmony that I speak of, will not be fully achieved in my Earthly lifetime. Nonetheless, there will continue to be great strides made among all of humankind as the Universe guides each one of us.

Through the "window" or opening that God has provided to me in this arena of future political and social harmony, I am made aware of the current energy of mistrust. This energy is one that has already begun to create discord among families, friends, neighbors, and coworkers, in many parts of the world. In some places that energy of mistrust has been fueled by the lies and manipulation of the very people who have been given Earthly political power to make laws, or to change laws. These are laws that affect not only the people who live and work within the boundaries of the Earthly lands that they govern, but also reverberate out into all parts of the universe.

No words, actions, or energy is ever released into the universe without every other particle of the universe being affected. Humankind, animals, plants, land, water, air—and perhaps most important—the very essence of the spirits we are, respond to all energy. All that I have just mentioned respond to all types of energy, whether positive or negative in intention. None of us live in a "safe zone," or in a social or political vacuum, where we can do as we please, consequences be damned.

My thoughts now return to the fact that I have never considered myself to be a person/spirit who is politically motivated. Typically, whenever a political ad on the television, radio, billboards, or yard signs comes into my line of sight, or within my range of hearing, I have long had the tendency to groan in disappointment. The words, actions, and energy of most politicians quickly become a blur of negative feeling energy. As a highly intuitive and psychic being, all I end up hearing is, "Blah, blah, blah. I'm so great and my opponents are so bad. I feel it's my duty to give you a list of the bad choices I feel *they* have made, both in his or her personal lives, as well as in his or her political careers!" That seems to always be followed up by a short piece of video, or a photo of the opposing candidates, along with quotes, (most of which are later revealed to be taken out of context.) I am never left with a feeling that "the voters" have all the facts necessary to make a sound political choice at the voting booths.

In some ways I have had an advantage when it comes to political candidates and all of the manipulating and posturing that many lean towards on the campaign trail. I was born with psychic abilities that allow me to see, hear, feel, smell, and even taste all that the Universe brings into my life path. And while my psychic gifts are wonderful, they do not take the place of the gift that every single one of us contains within us—our intuition. It is through the very intuition that connects each and every one of us to the

Universe, and to one another, that we are able to perceive the truth. And that includes the truth about politics, and the men and women whom we entrust to be our collective voice in the political arenas that govern our lives. Simply by choosing to pay close attention to any signs, or information that our Higher Power provides to us, through our innate gift of intuition, we are able to make informed decisions about "who" should be voted into office to do the best job of governing on our behalf.

I have always used my intuition to guide me in all areas of my life. At times, those feelings, those senses, are so light, and so subtle, that it would be easy to miss. However, I have found that God, angels, and spirit guides are pretty darn persistent, and never leave me stranded whenever I need help with any decision.

In the area of politics, I have never felt guided to pledge my allegiance to one specific political party, but rather I have felt the energy of the political candidates to determine who will get my vote. Do I feel the energy of truthfulness in that person? Is this a person/spirit whose intentions towards politics—and life in general—feel mostly positive to me? Is this a person whose energy feels negative . . . deceptive . . . egotistical?

Energy never lies, even when some people do. The real challenge for all of us is not "who to vote for," but is the test that the Universe gives us to *trust ourselves* to decipher our personal sense of political intuition. We must learn to *trust our personal intuitive senses*—even in the arena of politics—and to cast our votes accordingly. The topic of trusting oneself, when it comes to casting any political vote, is one is which I believe God has tested me in a rather unusual way. The test that I am referring to came through an unexpected, yet truly enlightening, spirit connection.

∞

The second political spirit encounter that I will share with my readers occurred in the early afternoon hours of October 25, 2002. Once again, I happened to be seated in my home office, alongside my then six-year-old granddaughter, Autumn. As I recall, it was a rather gloomy, gray day outdoors, with respect to the weather conditions. Inside my home, all was bright and sunny in our little corner of the world, as granddaughter and grandmother soon became immersed in our personal efforts to create art. There was a wonderful feeling of peace within my home office making it easy to relax into the flow of creative energy. I generally find that the deeper I go into my artistic endeavors, the quieter I am. Autumn had kept a slow, but steady, stream of chatter going for the better part of thirty minutes, when suddenly we both fell silent.

There was no apparent reason for our combined silence except that I would have to give credit to the Universe, to God, for guiding our spirits and minds to "be still" in those moments. I say that because I find that there are many such times in my life when it is best to be still . . . to be silent. It is often in those quiet moments when intuition speaks to us, and when the Universe chooses to bring a spirit through to connect with a psychically gifted person, such as Autumn or myself. A person who, like Autumn or myself, has been blessed with one or more of the many psychic abilities available that allow us to see, hear, feel, smell, or taste the energy of a spirit connection to whatever degree God deems necessary. I should add that a psychically gifted person does not control when or where a spirit connection occurs, nor can we control the information that is presented. We can only choose to learn and to grow in spiritual knowledge from these amazing experiences with spirit.

The silence in my small home office was finally broken by Autumn when she suddenly said, "Grandma, there's a spirit of a man here who wants to talk to you." I was not shocked by what my granddaughter told me as I was already fully aware of her psychic abilities. I had been guided to work with her from time-to-time, in an effort to help her better understand the spirit encounters that God had placed within her life path. My only response to Autumn was to instruct her to, "Ask God if this is a spirit that you are meant to talk to, and if so, then ask the man's spirit to tell you his name."

I had learned early on, through my personal psychic experiences, that there are many, many spirits who want to communicate with someone who is psychically gifted. However, it is best to keep healthy boundaries and only connect with those whom the Universe brings to us. Autumn sat quietly, for a moment, while she asked the question of God, and then waited for his answer. It was easy for Autumn to speak to God; she was a young child who had never been taught to fear her Higher Power, but rather she had been taught to trust her personal, intuitive connection to him. That is one of the joys of being a child is that they are born into a life with a heart that is generally "wide open" to connect with their Higher Power, with the Universe. While that open and trusting connection is often lost to our conscious awareness, as we grow older, the connection is never gone.

Autumn soon spoke aloud and said, "God says we are to talk to that man's spirit and so I did. His name is Paul." I thanked Autumn for her part in that spirit connection, but hesitated before I "spoke" to the waiting spirit in the room. I could not yet "see" the man's spirit, so I was not sure who Paul was, or why God had brought him into my home to speak with me on that gloomy and overcast day.

My conscious mind was trying to remember all of the men named "Paul" that I may have known in my life. The only one who seemed like a reasonable possibility was my ex-husband's deceased brother named Paul. At that particular time, I knew that Paul had been crossed over for more than six years. He had died of sudden cardiac arrest in Pittsburgh, Pennsylvania, where he had been in law enforcement for many years. As brother-in-laws and sister-in-laws go, I would say that Paul and I had gotten along fairly well, but I had not spoken to him, in the Earthly sense, since my divorce from his brother in 1994. I could not imagine why his spirit would want to pay me a visit, but I have learned to stay open to the Universe because there are always surprises around every corner.

As surprised as I would have been if that spirit *had* been my deceased brother-in-law, I was in for an even bigger shock. Within seconds the spirit in the room spoke to me, and revealed that his name was Paul Wellstone . . . Senator Paul Wellstone.

To say I was confused would be an understatement, as I could not imagine why God would have brought Minnesota Senator Paul Wellstone's spirit to me for a conversation. "God knows I'm not a political person/spirit even better than I know that, so what is the point of this sudden spirit visit?" I wondered. As that thought ran through my conscious mind, the visiting spirit allowed me to "see" him in the third eye region of my psychic sight.

Senator Paul Wellstone's spirit spoke rapidly, as he thanked me for coming out to see him speak several years prior at a union rally for the mechanics who worked at the Minneapolis International Airport. I told him I had actually forgotten about that rally, until he had just spoken about it, in spirit form. My mind drifted back to the rally and I did remember meeting him on that day. I recalled how enthusiastic he was in his efforts to speak to, and to listen to, all of the people who came to see him. I also realized, in those moments of recall, that I had never attended any other political campaign rally in my entire life. God must have felt it was pretty important for me to see, hear, and to feel Paul Wellstone's energy way back then, just as he was entering the political portion of his path in life.

The spirit of Paul Wellstone did not stop there, as he immediately began campaigning—not for himself, as I later realized—but for the Democrats to win the senate seat in the election that was mere days away. I had to laugh out loud, though I could not help but admire his enthusiasm! The spirit of any politician had never before approached me in an effort to convince me that his or her political party was the best choice in an upcoming election. Though I laughed, I still felt truly confused as to "why" Senator Paul Wellstone's spirit was standing in my home office, campaigning hard for my vote!

I told him that, while I appreciated his efforts and his enthusiasm for politics, I had to draw the line at politically endorsed spirits connecting with me, psychically, in an effort to sway my vote one way or the other. I respectfully declined to commit to voting Democratic, not because I wouldn't ever vote for a Democratic candidate, but because I vote for the person/spirit and never for the political party. I smiled at Senator Paul Wellstone's spirit as I told him that it was great to meet him, but I would be keeping my voting choice to myself.

I knew from all of the months of media coverage that Senator Paul Wellstone was running for reelection. I wished him success on his political journey. He smiled and thanked me for my time as he left my home, leaving me to sort out my thoughts on that particular spirit connection. I should add here that it is not only the deceased who can connect in spirit, as those of us who are still living an Earthly life can also connect during our times of soul travel. Nothing about Senator Paul Wellstone's spirit visit gave me any indication that he had left his Earthly life. That awareness would come to me in the way that God must have felt was necessary.

I sat quietly beside my granddaughter, Autumn, who was still busy painting watercolors. As hard as I tried I could not regain my own sense of creativity. Any sense of peaceful energy was completely shattered about ten minutes later when my oldest son, Brent, walked into my home office to share devastating news. Brent had just heard, through reliable media sources, that Senator Paul Wellstone's airplane was missing.

Senator Paul Wellstone had been travelling in a plane that morning, along with his wife, Sheila, and one of their three children—a grown and married daughter with a family of her own. In the news bulletin that Brent had heard, the search was on for the Senator's airplane, with hopes that all would be found alive. It was in that instant that the Universe allowed me to "feel" the energy that confirmed Senator Paul Wellstone had died. Later news reports confirmed that all three of the Wellstone family members had died in the plane crash, along with two pilots, the Senator's driver, and two of his campaign workers. Seven lives lost on that gloomy, gray day in a densely wooded area near the Eveleth, Minnesota airport.

I felt rather shaky as I discussed the spirit encounter that had just taken place in my modest home office between myself, my granddaughter, and a United States Senator from Minnesota who had just lost his Earthly life in a plane crash. Brent listened carefully to what I had to say, but neither of us could really wrap our conscious minds around what had just happened. This was one of those spirit connections that required a person to "step back in his or her spirit shoes" and to ask God to help explain things.

Even with all of the amazing psychic experiences that I have had, I was feeling such a loss for our country. I felt an enormous void in the political stream of energy that was meant to bring the United States of America to a greater sense of enlightenment. The fact that I did not personally know Senator Paul Wellstone, nor could I properly educate you on his political stance, does not matter. The loss I felt was about the loss of a man, of a spirit, who cared so deeply and so passionately about his country that he did not even let his own tragic death slow him down. Within a couple hours of his death, Paul Wellstone's spirit had convinced the Universe to "put him through" to connect with me, a highly gifted psychic medium, in an effort to pitch his political cause . . . just one more time. The phrase "politics as usual" would never mean the same thing to me again.

∞

Later that night I sat down to watch news coverage of the events that ended the life of a very positive and enthusiastic man. A man whose spirit God had guided to live his life as a United States Senator. That man, his dedicated wife, his beloved daughter, and four other people, were now part of the nightly news. Not because of any new political statement, but because those people's lives were all fated to end on that dismal October day.

I found myself once again connecting with the spirit of Senator Paul Wellstone as I thanked him for his political service to our country. His intentions felt sure-footed, and mostly positive, which is all each of us can hope to be in our own life paths. I got to "see" that big grin of his, one last time, as he told me he had lived his life, and had experienced death, in the ways that God had intended. He said he was at peace. Senator Paul Wellstone's spirit told me that his wife Sheila's spirit was by his side, and for that he was grateful.

The Senator's spirit then promptly became a father in his energy, as he looked more thoughtful about the death of his daughter. He felt sorry for the children that God had placed in her care, as they would certainly miss her. But he also seemed to know that her spirit would "mother them from heaven," as best she could.

I felt the strength of his family ties, and not only to the two sons who were left to carry on the legacy of his work. God also allowed me to feel the sense of family ties that resonated from the senator's spirit towards his extended family, towards his working staff, and the sense of family that Senator Paul Wellstone's spirit generated towards all of humankind. I knew I had been given a gift that day when the Universe allowed me to better understand one of our Earthly politicians through spirit connections.

And as the spirits of two deeply committed politicians—Abraham and Paul—now work with our Higher Power to heal themselves, in heaven, the world continues to move—ever so slowly—towards a time when humankind truly *will* work together peaceably. That time of peace will come to us when each person/spirit brings his or her strengths to the forefront, while respect for one another's differences prevails.

CHAPTER FOUR

Once Upon a Time

As children, we all loved to hear a story that began with the words "once upon a time." We cherish the memories of any adult who took time, out of his or her busy schedule, to read aloud to us. The subject matter of the story was not really the important part of those wonderful childhood memories, but the fact that an adult was willing to indulge us, with the time and energy necessary to give a good story its wings, made us feel special. We felt as though we were the most important person in the world—for at least as long as it took to read that particular story!

I remember the times, when certain adults, would read me a story in such a way, that it allowed me to feel as though I had become a part of the story. The words that I heard spoken aloud gave my conscious mind the ability to visualize whatever was happening in the story. And if my adult reader happened to be the kind of person who was willing to lend different voices to each character in the story, I found my interest was heightened significantly. Whenever those kinds of story-telling sessions would end, I always found myself wanting more. But for the most part, I generally accepted that I had agreed to a bargain of one bedtime story in exchange for no fuss in getting to bed.

As a young child, my family had a large book of popular, old, bedtime stories; some had morals to them, and some were just fanciful writings of people who lived long ago. I loved the fact that so many wonderful stories were all bound together in one amazing book! My older sister and I also had some Little Golden books, which I also loved to read, but they did not hold the same power to draw me in or to open up my imagination. On one hand, I loved to look at the illustrations that covered the pages of most children's books, yet I also enjoyed listening to the stories as my father read to me from the large book of bedtime stories. I could close my eyes as I listened to my father read a story and almost instantly I could "see" the story in my mind.

I do not really have any memories of my mother reading aloud to me as a young child, but I do recall my father sitting upon the edge of my bed, as he chose a bedtime story to read aloud for my older sister, Debbie, and me. We had another sister, Barbara, who was still just a baby, so any time spent with one of our busy parents was important. I was about four or five years old, at that point in time, and enjoyed that bedtime ritual immensely.

That period of my life did not last long, as another sister, Lisa, joined the family when I was six-and-one-half years old. With four young children to care for—and a fifth soon to come—our parents were kept quite busy. Nonetheless, the seed to be a good reader had already been planted, deep within me. I had already begun to read some children's books on my own, and found that I could ask my older sister, Debbie, for help if I got stuck on a new or more difficult word.

For myself, as it is for many people, I found the Universe guiding me to assume the responsibility of being a storyteller long before I became an adult. Even as a young child, I found that my sister, Debbie, would often ask me to tell her a story in the quiet sanctuary of our shared bedroom. I had a knack for thinking up stories and remembering them, so I would add a few more details to the stories each night. One of our favorites was a story that I called "The Lonely Little Bear©." Many evenings my last thoughts as a child were the words of a story that I had just spun aloud for my sister, Debbie, and me.

There is no doubt in my mind that words, reading, and storytelling, have always had a significant place in my life path. Already as a young child, I found that the time that any adult invested into reading aloud to me, soon transferred to an overwhelming urge to learn to read for myself. The more I read, the more I wanted to read. I soon found myself reading aloud to my younger sisters, cousins, and many of the younger children that lived in the neighborhood.

The first several times that I read aloud I felt self-conscious, almost as if I was being judged in some way. Rather than to succumb to my fears, I remembered how I felt whenever an adult or older child would read to me. I never cared if they had to pause occasionally to sound out a word. I didn't mind if they lost their place in the story for an instant, because I was so grateful for the time they were giving me. Those memories of being read to as a child gave me the courage to do the same thing for other children. And as soon as any of those children became good readers, I encouraged them to read aloud to others. Without any thought on my part, I now know that God had intuitively guided me into the part of becoming a role model—for children of all ages—to become good readers, and motivated writers.

∞

Role models in any positive form are vastly important in all of our lives. Even now, as a grandmother, I am prone to perpetuate the example of reading alone, as well as reading to others. From an early age, I witnessed my mother reading the newspaper each day, along with an occasional book or magazine. Many evenings I noticed my father, seated comfortably in the den of our home, with his feet propped up on a hassock; his focus on the pages of whatever book he was currently reading. Though my parents rarely discussed what they were reading, I do feel that they left an indelible impression upon me, with regards to the importance of reading.

In addition to being "reading role models by example," my parents were always encouraging my older sister, and me, to check out library books from our school library, and to read, read, read! Every week our teachers would send home a list of new words to learn how to spell, and my parents expectations did not allow for anything less.

Growing up with five children in the family allowed for fairly regular visits to doctors, dentists, and even an occasional trip to a hospital emergency room. At every doctor or dental appointment my parents expected us to sit quietly, and to behave. In that way, a good book to read was like having a friend to keep you company. If a medical office had a subscription to the Highlights magazine for children, I would snatch it up, and do all of the word puzzles! As I grew older, I found myself drawn to reading the Reader's Digest, not only for the funny jokes or stories, but also to learn the meanings of new words that were on that month's list. To this day I stay open to learning new words, as I love the fact that language seems never-ending.

By the time I hit double-digits in Earthly years, I was a voracious reader. I read books, magazines, newspapers—even recipes and billboards! My skills as a storyteller became stronger, as I had begun to realize that no good story could be told without each character having a voice of his or her own. I often found I was in big demand as a babysitter for neighborhood families. I could keep the children amused with stories and characters that I could invent on a moments notice. I loved to read their favorite children's books aloud to them, as it was interesting to me to see which books each child picked as his or her favorite.

∞

The books I have read throughout my life have varied greatly in subject matter. I have read my share of fiction books, and have enjoyed the stories of adventure, of love, of hope, and I loved to solve mysteries! And of course, I have quietly cheered on whomever I felt was "the good guy" in any story. Like most people, I was always glad to read of some villainous person getting his or her comeuppance!

I have never limited myself to just one genre of books, but as I have grown older, I have found myself drawn more to works of nonfiction. I have discovered that as I grow in Earthly years, and in wisdom, there is no fictional book that can match the true-life stories that the Universe guides each of us to live through. I suspect that is one of the motivating factors behind God's guidance, for me, to write about the truth of my life—as a psychic medium, as a woman, wife, mother, grandmother, and so forth. I smile, as I acknowledge the fact, that no work of fiction could ever come close to what I have been blessed to experience as the truth of my life.

The words that I write, and the stories that I share, all "ring true" to our collective inner selves, because each of us has the ability to recognize truth in that way. We do not merely "hear the truth" of a person's words, nor do we simply "read words" to know that they are true. Instead, the very spirits we have, within our physical bodies, are designed with a built-in truth meter that does not ever lie. The "truth meter" I speak of is the gift of intuition that our Higher Power has given to every one of us. Our intuition will always provide us with all that we need, in any given moment of our lives.

That powerful gift of intuition, or "truth meter," gives us the ability to discern between a person who is just "telling us a make-believe story" versus a person—like myself—who is sharing the real stories of his or her life. The phrase "once upon a time" has no real place in any of the chapters I write, as it leads a person to believe that what is about to be told *must* be a fairy tale, right? Well, my readers, I can only encourage you to read on—and as you do—allow *your* intuition to measure the truth of *my* words.

∞

Once upon a time . . . the weatherman had predicted another hot, humid, July day in Minnesota. No psychic abilities or strong intuition were necessary for him to forecast a very typical day of weather for those of us who call Minnesota "home" during the month of July. Yet, the very instant I opened my eyes, to view the daylight that had already entered the bedroom, I remembered why this July day would be so different from all others. The date was July 6, 2001, a date that should have signified the twentieth birthday for my son, Brady . . . but he was no longer with us. The Earthly clock and calendar had officially stopped for him when he made the choice to end his life on December 31, 2000. At the age of nineteen and one half years the clock stopped ticking, and Brady would never again smile upon a birthday cake filled with brightly glowing candles. I would never again see the twinkle in Brady's eyes, as he paused briefly to make a wish, before his breath gently blew out all of those lit candles.

I felt the warm tears as they slid down my cheeks and fell into my ears. I had been laying flat on my back, remembering what was far too painful too think about, but I could not help myself. The very date, on the calendar in my mind, would not allow me to ignore the importance of the day.

My eyes closed, as if that could prevent any more tears, but of course, that did not help. Tears flowed quietly, and softly, as my spirit, mind, and body merged into one helpless being. Part of me wanted to stay in bed and let July 6th pass by without a word. That same part of me wanted no gestures to remind me, or any of Brady's loved ones, that he was gone. However, the stronger—and perhaps more resilient part of me—was willing to get up and face the day. I could almost hear the inner voice of my own spirit saying, "We WILL get up and face this day—tears be damned!"

With no any further thoughts I pulled myself up, and out of bed, to begin living through that first birthday without Brady. As quickly as I began moving, I felt my son's spirit enter the room. Instantly I could smell his favorite cologne, Acqua Di Gio by Giorgio Armani. I had learned long ago, that I have the psychic gift within me that allows me to smell whatever scent, or scents, any spirit tries to convey to me. I am also a person who is acutely affected by the sense of smell. Smells can evoke memories and emotions in me, to such a degree, that those triggers can be powerful in leading me towards a positive experience in my life path. A single scent can also effectively stop me from stepping into harm's way. Yes, the physical and the psychic sense of smell is a powerful one, indeed.

The sudden appearance of Brady's spirit, and the joy of smelling "him," along with his cologne, brought me such a moment of joy that it is hard to put into words. Think of that particular spirit connection in the same way that you feel when a person you love, and care about, walks into a room, and you take in his or her entire essence through your sense of smell.

Each person has a very distinct and personal odor, or scent. We have the ability to recognize that scent even if we were blindfolded, or unable to see the person with our physical eyes. Most people add perfumes, colognes, deodorants, or scented shampoos, to the mix, yet none of those chemical scents can mask the person or spirit that we smell.

If we have had mostly positive experiences with a person, we tend to relate to his or her scent with a positive response within our spirits, minds, and bodies. However, if our past experiences with any person have left a dark or negative imprint upon us, we tend to cringe, or pull away from anything that reminds us of how he or she smelled. All of this applies whether a person is still living an Earthly life, or whether they have died and crossed over. For me, the opportunity to experience the scent of my son, Brady, in the early hours of his birthday, was priceless. It was powerfully healing, and seemed to bolster my resolve to make something positive from that day.

∞

Soon after entering the bedroom, Brady's spirit began to speak to me through the audio portion of my psychic gifts. The audio psychic ability, or "gift of hearing spirits" as I call it, allows me to "hear" all that is spoken as thoughts in my mind. I should add that, on occasion, I do hear the actual voice of a spirit speaking. When this phenomenon occurs, it registers to me as being heard through my physical ears, and seamlessly translates into words that I "hear" in my brain. When this happens it sounds the same, to me, as when any living person speaks.

Brady's message to me in the morning hours of July 6, 2001, was that he did not want me to be sad on what should have been his twentieth birthday. My son's spirit also did not want his two brothers, Brent and Blake, to spend the day depressed. While that sounds like a great idea, I knew that accomplishing all of that was easier said than done. Nonetheless, Brady suggested that my husband, Bob, and I, host a small party for a few people. This was a small group of people whom Brady felt might be helped by facing his birthday together. His spirit had the awareness that a small party would be far better than for all of us to sit home—alone—with our sad thoughts and heavy hearts.

As my conscious mind absorbed all that was transmitted by Brady's spirit, I found myself "speaking" to my son in my thoughts. I told Brady that I would do what he suggested, but that first I needed to go to the cemetery to visit his grave. I had a strong sense that a trip to his gravesite was really more about what I needed, rather than what my son's spirit would gain from my visit to the spot where his physical body had been interred. Brady's spirit left me alone with my thoughts, and soon after I began making phone calls to begin preparations for a birthday celebration for my deceased son.

Every person that I felt intuitively guided to call on that hot July day responded positively. They, too, felt the need to gather together to remember Brady on his birthday. My husband, Bob, felt that we should have the party later in the day so that we could make a small bonfire. Bob suggested we roast hot dogs, and toast marshmallows for chocolate smores, as Brady loved all of those things nearly as much as he loved a good party. Those suggestions all felt really good to me. As the birthday celebration plans were being made, I could, literally, feel all of the heaviness of the day being lifted off of my shoulders.

I knew that Brady was never going to be a part of our lives in the same physical sense that he had been. I also felt that I had accepted his death, but the healing from such a deep level of grief takes time and effort. I had made my own choice to begin healing in the immediate hours and days after Brady's death had occurred. In those earliest moments of grief, I had felt such darkness, and a level of pain, that I had never known existed until my son's death. I knew that I did not want to succumb to that darkness. And now—on this first birthday without my son—I knew that the Universe had brought my son's spirit to me, in an effort to aid in my choice to heal, and to help others do the same.

∞

The trip I took to the cemetery that day was filled with symbolic gestures; ones that I hoped would help my heart to mend. I hoped Brady's spirit would recognize, and find value in, those same gestures as he worked to heal on the other side, in heaven.

Bob drove me to Acacia Park Cemetery in Mendota Heights, Minnesota, not because I couldn't drive myself there, but because he felt it was important to accompany me. My husband felt instinctively that he needed to be a support person for me, in those moments. My inner self guided me strongly to time our visit to the cemetery to match the exact time of day when Brady had come into his life. We arrived at his gravesite promptly at 2:32 p.m. (CDT).

Along the way we picked up a few items that I felt were imperative to bring along to Brady's gravesite, on that particular date. There were three white roses to symbolize Brady, and his two brothers, who I knew would be forever linked to one another through a bond of love that only brothers can know. I had also chosen some yellow flowers that looked as though they may have belonged to the tiger lily species; I really don't know. I was drawn to them because I felt Brady's spirit around me as I looked at them in the flower shop. In that way, those yellow flowers seemed to be the right choice.

I placed those yellow flowers, along with the three white roses, into the built-in vase on my son's gravestone. As I did that I could not help but wonder what I would have given to Brady for his twentieth birthday, had he lived. I had to smile, through my tears, because I knew darn well I would *not* have bought him flowers!

Two other people, who also loved Brady, had been to his gravesite earlier that day. Each had left her own choice of flowers, along with small, handwritten cards to commemorate his absence on that day. One was a bouquet of fragrant red roses from one of his aunts; the other was a bright gathering of red carnations with two white ones to symbolize whatever that person felt the need to express at that time.

I did not have to voice out loud what my heart knew. Had Brady lived, neither of those persons would have given him flowers for his birthday. They knew him well enough to know he would have spent his birthday doing something outdoors, with lots of activity involved. "Hmmm," I thought to myself, "I'll bet he would have gone camping, or maybe canoeing with his buddies. Or perhaps Brady would have chosen to go waterskiing on a lake near our home, followed by a barbeque party with a whole bunch of his friends." Yes, *that* would have been his twentieth birthday, I was certain of it!

The drifting of my thoughts was brought back into clear focus as I, once again, looked upon my son's gravesite. Bob and I had also purchased a couple of brightly colored Mylar balloons that a pleasant store clerk had filled with helium. Bright balloons with messages that said, "Happy Birthday!" and "I LOVE YOU!" had accompanied those white roses and yellow tiger lilies to the cemetery. Bob tied those bright balloons to the base of the grave stone vase; I stood back, allowing my more creative and artistic self to voice its opinion.

"That looks good now, thanks Bob," I heard myself say quietly and calmly. But inside, I felt my spirit's energy bouncing around, uncertain as to what to do next. I wanted to stay calm as I allowed my eyes to take in my son's birthday decorated gravesite, because it really was a beautiful tribute to him. And the responsible leader, and role model, part of me certainly did not want to make a scene in the cemetery on that hot July day. However, there was a bigger part of me that felt an overwhelming need to "speak the truth" of all that I was feeling.

My conscious mind did not have to make the choice. Without hesitation, my spirit within spilled forth all of the grief, the pain, and the heart wrenching emotions, that come to a mother who stands at her child's gravesite to celebrate a birthday. Hot tears stung my cheeks, as uncontrollable sobs caused my chest to heave involuntarily. My legs weakened to the point I had to sit down next to Brady's gravestone. My husband, Bob, took one look at me, and walked quickly to our car to retrieve a box of badly needed tissues. He returned immediately, and stood nearby, as I spoke aloud, both to him and to the spirit of my deceased son.

Like most people, Bob has a very compassionate heart, but he also realizes that there are times in life when all of us need a person to be our sounding board. A "sounding board" is a person who simply listens, without judgment, as we bring forth our deepest thoughts and feelings. In those moments, at Brady's gravesite, I needed someone to *listen to me* as I spoke the words that needed to be released from my spirit's heart. It was not really necessary for anyone to engage in conversation with me, as I knew there was not one thing that anyone could say, in those very moments, that could take away my pain, or heal a mother's broken heart.

There is an old saying that goes something like this: "When we are born we cry as all around us smile, so let us live that when we die we may smile as all around us cry." I do not know who first uttered those words, but I felt the wisdom of the message. I remembered that phrase, because, to me, it described Brady's birth and his death quite well. I felt the truth of that old saying, even as I sobbed, unabashedly, at the foot of my son's grave.

Through the intuition of my inner self in those moments, I also knew that I did not have to "be strong," as the mother who always tried hard to lead her sons, and many others, through the mucky, mire called grief. My own feelings needed to be released or I could not go forward in my own healing process. On that day, at that specific time, I needed to be at the very site where my son's choice to die had brought him. I knew it was the perfect time to tell him that I have never felt such pain. It was important that I voice the very words, that would let my son's spirit know, *that I would give anything to have him back in his physical body*—smiling and teasing me—because that was his very nature.

My words expressed the love and loss that I felt, but also the pain and anger. The death of a child, by any means, and at any age, feels grossly unfair. And it makes a parent feel angry. We often say, "Why *me*? Why do I have to bury my son (or daughter)? Why couldn't you let my child live?" as we look upon the heavens for even the tiniest semblance of understanding. It is not as though we want anyone else's child to die; we don't. We simply do not want to be the parent who has to settle for placing flowers, and bright balloons, at the gravesite of our child, instead of hosting a *real* party, with *real* birthday gifts, for our *real live child*.

I do not remember all that I said out loud to God, to Brady's spirit, and to my husband, Bob, who stood patiently by as I expressed myself in Acacia Park Cemetery on July 6, 2001. But I do remember the sense of relief I felt when I was done. I was emotionally spent, yet I also felt a deep sense of cleansing as I blew my nose, and wiped away the last tears of those moments. As my right hand steadied my uneasy legs, Bob took hold of my left hand, and helped me to my feet, holding me in a close embrace for a couple of minutes; I had nothing more to say.

∞

The rest of Brady's twentieth birthday celebration was filled with more tears, lots of laughter, and an abundance of hugs. It felt good to share all of that with a few of the many people who loved Brady. The impromptu birthday party for Brady was held at our home, the very place where my son had chosen to die. Also in attendance were my two remaining sons, Brent and Blake, who seemed grateful for the opportunity to remember the brother, who linked them to one another, in a casual gathering among close family and friends.

No subject was off limits in our discussions of Brady, not on that day—nor on any other day, for that matter. The talk among all who were there would range from bursts of laughter, as each of us shared some of our best "Brady moments," to the quiet and profound silence that came to us when we all stopped to contemplate the choice to die that Brady had made six months prior. I could sense that it was difficult, for everyone who knew Brady, to grasp the notion that *he* would be a person to choose death over life.

As a mother, the suicide death of one of your children is nearly inconceivable, but in my work as a psychic medium I have come to understand that every family, every person, will be touched by the action and energy of "self-murder" that suicide brings into the lives of those who remain. The idea that my son would have chosen to end the life of *anyone* seems preposterous, even now, but the idea that Brady could choose—and did choose—to take the life of my beloved son, required a leap of faith to accept. The idea that Brady could take the life of my very smart, funny, good-looking, physically active, hardworking, musically gifted, and yes, substance challenged addict, son, is enough to force a mother to step back in her spirit shoes so that she can better understand and accept a most difficult life experience.

It was clear to me, at the time of Brady's death, and the same sense returned to me during the birthday gathering on July 6, 2001, that no one who knew Brady—in any capacity—ever expected to feel the grief of his death by suicide. Those who truly knew my son probably would not have been surprised if Brady had died young, in some other fashion, such as a snowmobile accident, or from a skiing accident. My son was a spirit who always pushed the limits, and loved to be active.

I had learned, at a young mother, that I could only choose to do my best as Brady's mom. I felt, instinctively, that I had to trust the Universe to keep him safe from harm. Brady was always the little boy who had to climb the tree as high as his older brother Brent did, even as I stood on the ground warning him to "Stop! Don't climb any higher, Brady!" I have to smile now, as even in those times when Brady would make a choice that would cause my heart to beat fast, or would fill me with a sudden sense of fear for his safety, I *loved* being Brady's mom! Brady was a person, a spirit, who really *lived* every minute of his life. I was reminded of that in the late evening hours of July 6, 2001, as we all sat quietly gazing into the hypnotic glow of a bonfire that had been lit in Brady's honor, just as he would have wanted.

Throughout the day I had already felt, heard, seen, and even smelled the essence of Brady's spirit, but as I sat near the fire pit I was aware of my son's spirit in what felt like magnified proportions. I could feel Brady "hug" me as he whispered in my ear, "You are the very best mom that God could have ever brought me into a life to be raised by. I want to thank you for all that you did." Of course, those words spoken by Brady's spirit brought a rush of warmth to my heart, and the biggest teardrops imaginable were running down my cheeks.

In my own thoughts I silently talked to Brady's spirit and told him that no matter how long he had lived, or how the Universe had guided him to experience his death, I was eternally grateful that he was my son. As soon as those words left my thoughts, I felt my son's spirit acknowledge them as his spirit hugged me tighter. Next I psychically "saw" his energy flow around all of the people who had gathered, around the fire, to share in what would have been his twentieth birthday celebration. The best way I can describe what I saw is that it was similar to the light show that is produced in the sky that weather predictors call "Northern Lights."

Brady's spirit changed color rapidly, and seemed to rise and fall, twist and turn, in a way that allowed him to connect with the spirit energy of each and every person seated around the campfire. But perhaps more important than that the fact that I saw, and felt, his spirit, was that I felt the most intense energy of unconditional love from Brady's spirit towards every one of us. It is hard to describe how wonderful that felt, as it was an energy that was felt so deep within my spirit's heart that it exploded. That explosion of energy felt like a wonderful current of "electric love" throughout my entire spirit, mind, and body. I found it hard to speak for a few moments, as I just needed to "be" in the energy of Brady's unconditional love.

∞

Could every single person see, hear, feel, or smell Brady's spirit in the way that the Universe had allowed me to experience my spirit connections with him on that hot July day? The answer is no, probably not, as each of us is unique in how we perceive spirit experiences. That said, I do recall many of the family members and friends at the party did express his or her specific awareness that Brady's spirit had been making efforts to connect with them. Most of them appeared, to me, to be open to such moments. Perhaps that is why the Universe, whom I call God, guided me to stay open in my heart, on my son's first birthday after his death. I am certain God knew that those who attended our party would receive wonderful gifts of spirit connection that could help to heal grieving hearts, and to open conscious minds.

In just one day I personally experienced countless profound, and deeply healing, spirit connections with my son Brady's spirit. I now understand why my Higher Power guided me to write this chapter, and to share it with my readers, who in turn will be guided to tell others.

In the way that only our Higher Power understands, that young man's spirit truly needed to assist in the healing process of his mother. That help was badly needed so that his mother could follow her unique life path, one that began when she was a very young child.

The Universe has worked hard to continue to guide the young man's spirit, who often assists his mother, but now as a guardian angel. The young man's spirit, who once chose to die, has now found a great sense of purpose. He has seen that his mother lives a life path in which the Universe requires her to *"Write so that others may heal!"*

The young man watches closely as his mother works hard to respect her life's mission, and to live her life in such a way as the Universe deems is so. The young man's spirit seems happy that his mother's work and her books will teach others about psychic abilities, and the immeasurable value of spirit connections in each of our lives. The young man's spirit has expressed his admiration for a mother who chose to live life with a open heart and a keen mind, always accepting of a day that might reveal the next story that begins with "once upon a time."

Of course, the young man's spirit will always be "my son, Brady," and I am the mother whose spirit has a lifetime of stories and experiences to write about. As a seasoned adult, I acknowledge the importance of all of the reading, as well as the storytelling experiences that the Universe had guided me through as a child. All of it helped to prepare me for my work as a writer, and as a person who is willing to share the unfeigned stories of her life. The heart wrenching stories of spirit connections with loved ones who have crossed over, are not exclusive to my life. But my willingness to describe these events, and to share them publically, is unique.

It is my fondest wish that another person will become inspired by my life stories, and as a result, he or she will learn to not only read well, but also be willing to write the truths of his or her life path. Remember, *our stories* are the stories that will serve to teach generations to come. Our willingness to speak the truths of our lives is the foundation upon which a more positive, compassionate, and accepting universe can be built.

CHAPTER FIVE

The King and I

There are times in each of our lives when God guides us to do something, or to take a step towards some action in our own life path, that leaves us feeling confused, even dumbfounded. Writing this chapter was one of those moments for me. I don't get sick very often, but a few days before I was intuitively guided to begin writing this particular chapter I had begun to get the same sore throat and bad cough that two of my granddaughters had. The night before my writing began I found that I could barely sleep as a headache, body aches and a general feeling of "Just take me *now*, God!" joined my other symptoms. Yes, it was one of those days when a person feels so sick they just don't care what else is going on in the world *"because nobody can possibly feel as lousy as I do"* is the only thought that runs through his or her mind!

I have shared the truth of how bad I felt during the writing process of this chapter because it is a great example of one of those times in my life when God has guided such strong inspiration through to me, and yet I am baffled. My gut instincts tell me that a great number of my readers can find solace in knowing that they have not been alone in those times of life when the Universe kept pushing and prodding them to *"Move forward! Keep going!"* even when all we may feel like doing is catering to our illness of that particular moment.

In my case I felt certain that my Higher Power knew how poorly I was feeling on that day. Why did God insist on pushing me so hard to *"Get out of bed . . . take your shower . . . eat something . . . and type out this chapter of your book"*?

The reminder came to me as I laid in bed, trying hard to ignore the voice of God as he tried even harder to stir me to action on that cool winter day, that God has always guided me strongly through my intuition; those unmistakable gut instincts that we all have. He has also made it clear to me that my work as a psychic medium is unique, and that I do not have regular nine-to-five hours like other working people often do. I sighed as I rolled out of bed on that dismally gray March day in 2009 and declined any opportunity to look in the mirror. I knew I felt lousy and didn't care to confirm that diagnosis with a look in the mirror, as some things just don't need to be mirrored back at us for a second opinion!

In the warmth of the shower I closed my eyes and allowed God to give me whatever images, words, feelings, and sense of the situation that he chose to. Immediately God conveyed all of the reminders that would lead me to write this specific chapter for my book. The title of this chapter came clearly to me, as did all of the parts of this chapter. Again I asked, "Why now? Why in these very moments when I am so sick?" God replied, *"Because it is time in your own life path. All that you are feeling in your physical body is a healing release that I have helped your inner self with. This too shall pass. You will feel much better if you occupy yourself with a sense of positive purpose . . . you always do!*" Yes, that rang true to me, deep inside. And so I began writing this chapter in March 2009, even though I would later come to realize that this chapter would become a part of my second book that would not be completed or published until 2012. I guess God knew I could accomplish something positive in those moments that could serve a greater purpose later on, at a point in my life and in my work, that only he could measure the value of as he also determined the sense of perfection in timing.

∞

In early July 2005 my husband, Robert (Bob) Dedeker, and I were both getting strong guidance from God through our own intuition that we should take a short trip to Las Vegas, Nevada. Bob and I had each been to Las Vegas, Nevada only one other time in our lives and that was nearly six years prior. It had also been during the winter so leaving the cold of Minnesota for three or four days had been delightful. But in 2005 we realized that our Higher Power wanted us to go to that hot desert city in July . . . *July?* As my husband and I discussed the solid guidance we were each receiving from God, I reminded him that I don't do well in high heat, especially since I suffered from heat stroke back in 1988. Recent news coverage had focused on some areas of the country, including Las Vegas, that were experiencing record high temperatures. Why would we have possibly needed to go there at that time?

We each took the time to talk to our Higher Power about this guidance and to ask any questions that came to our minds. In spite of my own strong psychic abilities, I always get the guidance in my own life path the same way that everyone does—through the intuition of my inner self in all ways that God provides it. As I sat quietly and listened, watched, and felt whatever the Universe was giving me, I became aware that there was psychic work in Las Vegas that God wanted me to do. I was not being told who was involved, or when any of the messages and information would come to me. I only knew that there were people there that God was requesting my help in relaying messages to.

This is actually very common in my work as a psychic medium. Quite often God will guide me to a person or a location, and then suddenly—without warning—the psychic work begins! Within that short trip to Las Vegas, Nevada both Bob and I understood that we would get to enjoy a brief vacation, as well as we would be able to experience whatever the Universe felt that we each personally needed to at that time in our life paths. My work as a psychic medium would complete the necessity for our travel at that time.

The next question was financial in nature when Bob asked me, "How can we afford a trip to Las Vegas at this particular time?" I pondered that question as well but shared with Bob the fact that God was guiding me clearly through my intuition. The messages from the Universe were easily shown and told to me. I shared with Bob that my own intuitive sense was strong in that our trip to Las Vegas, Nevada would cost no more than $500.00 for our travel and lodging. The Universe had made it abundantly clear to me that we were to take another $300.00 for food and a little bit of gaming. Beyond that, all I knew from God's guidance was that we had to choose to trust that God will provide all that we need, as we needed it. We looked at each other and I shrugged my shoulders as I smiled. The look on my husband's face told me that, while he knew I paid close attention to my personal intuition that I receive from my Higher Power, a trip to Las Vegas seemed a bit of a stretch to Bob's conscious mind.

Fifteen minutes later we were sitting in the office of a local travel agent, facing her as I explained that we wanted to book between three and four days travel to Las Vegas, Nevada within the next week or so. My words came easily as I explained to the travel agent that I was a psychic medium and my own guidance was telling me that we could get the airfare and hotel accommodations for the two of us for no more than $500.00. Our travel agent was a seasoned traveler herself and good at her job. Over the years we had taken a few trips to other destinations and she had proven herself to be more than competent in her job. She looked from me to Bob, and then shook her head back and forth in the common way as if to express, "No, that's just not possible."

The travel agent began to speak to me slowly and deliberately, almost as if I had some sort of brain injury that would not allow me to comprehend what she was saying. I didn't take it personal as she said, "You are not going to find any type of deal to Las Vegas in your price range. Not now, and probably not ever again. Those prices haven't been available for a few years now." Again, I explained that my own intuition was strong, and that I was also getting psychically that she would be able to find us that $500.00 deal.

For several minutes our travel agent stopped speaking to us and worked diligently at her computer. Hotel and airfares kept popping up on her computer screen as Bob and I strained to view the cost of those deals. The travel agent began muttering under her breath, speaking the details and costs of various travel promotions in a whisper to herself. Finally she turned the computer screen towards us, as if to prove once and for all, that the $500.00 travel package deal did not exist. I could see for myself that all of the current travel deals were priced in the $639.00 to $850.00 range for the lowest prices. There were many travel packages priced higher though nothing for $500.00 was making itself known.

As the travel agent paused in her search for a moment, Bob looked at me and asked, "What now?" As he spoke those words I was already talking to God in my head and listening for my guidance. The answer came quickly and quietly. *"Trust in my guidance to you. The deal will present itself."* I leaned over to tell Bob what I had just gotten from my Higher Power. My husband raised his eyebrows at me and smiled nervously as if to say, "I sure hope so!"

Suddenly the travel agent said, "I'm going try one last thing." and typed a few keystrokes on her computer keyboard. Instantly our deal appeared on her screen. Our hotel and airline tickets for four nights and five days in Las Vegas, Nevada . . . $499.99! Our travel agent looked stunned at first glance, but then smiled broadly as she now turned to face us with the newly found travel package. As she explained the terms of that deal to us we both felt immediately that this was it! The hotel was only one short block from several of the newer, luxurious hotels and casinos. And although it was an older hotel with a small casino, it had good ratings, and was directly across the street from the entrance to the monorail system. We could leave within days for this mystery trip of ours!

∞

Just days later Bob and I found ourselves exiting the doors at McCarran International Airport in Las Vegas, Nevada. We had our luggage in tow as we stepped outdoors and into the shuttle bus, taxi, and limousine area. Per the terms of our travel arrangements, Bob and I needed to acquire our own transportation to the hotel. Both of us were smiling and happy as we stepped out—until we took that first breath of scorching hot desert air! For an instant I found myself speechless—and that doesn't happen often! Whoa! Hold on for just a minute! *This* is where God thought we needed to spend some time? I glanced over to Bob and saw that he was giving me a look that said, "Are you going to be able to handle this heat?" At that moment, I really did not think I could function well there. I don't recall the exact temperature on that day, but it was well over 100 degrees each day of our trip, with one of the days reaching around 116 degrees. Now, I don't care what climate a person is used to living in—that is hot!

We wandered over to the nearest shuttle bus and were told that one had just departed, but we could take a seat on the bench. The nice man assured us that there would be only a short wait for the next shuttle bus that could take us to the hotel and casino district. I politely asked just how long that meant, in real time, before we would actually reach our hotel because I was concerned about being out in the heat for long. The man's reply was, "Probably about an hour by the time the shuttle drops you off at your hotel because it has to make the rounds to several other hotels first." My face fell; I felt that I needed some consistent air conditioning before that.

My own intuition guided me strongly to go over to the limousine departure stand, so I shared that with Bob. He questioned me on whether or not we had the cost of a limousine ride in our meager vacation budget. Before I could answer my husband, we were approached by one of the limousine drivers. He was a pleasant younger man who immediately offered us the opportunity to ride in a luxury stretch limousine. As tempted as I was to just say "yes," and ignore my own good sense, I knew better. The Universe was still giving me clear guidance about our situation so I paid close attention. As I looked over to my right I saw a sign that listed the cost of the private rides in the various sizes of limousines. Both Bob and I knew right away that we could not afford the price of the large limousine that the chauffeur had offered us.

Now I have to add here that most people tend to get embarrassed if they find themselves without a lot of money, however that had been a condition of my life for so long now that I accepted it with grace—God's grace. I have long ago learned—and have truly accepted—that if I am supposed to have a certain amount of money at any time in my own life path, then God will provide that to me in whatever ways that he feels is necessary. As long as I pay close attention to my own intuitive guidance from my Higher Power I always find that this guidance includes anything I need to experience with regards to money and finances, as well as all other things. This spiritual understanding about money has been truly freeing for me, and for my husband, Bob, too. Oh sure, there have been plenty of times when we wished that we had more money, but the point is, we have always found that our true needs for our own life paths are provided—even when we are not always aware that we have that need. We have learned to keep our list of "wants" at a reasonable level, and yet, we still have our larger dreams that keep us moving forward.

I turned back to face the kind limousine driver and explained to him that we simply could not afford the price. He was not rude or haughty with us. Instead he suggested that we could still get a limousine ride with him *if* we were willing to go in one of the smaller luxury cars! That nice young man smiled at us and said that he wasn't busy right now and he would be happy to drive us for a discounted price. The cost he quoted us was only five dollars more than we would have had to pay for the shuttle service for the two of us. We thanked him and happily accepted his gracious offer to ride in air-conditioned comfort.

On the short and very direct ride to our hotel, I was given the psychic information from an angel to pass on a couple of brief messages to the young driver. This may sound strange, but I find that the opportunities to do my psychic work are made easy by the Universe. God always holds the doors open; all I have to do is pay attention and to have no fear as I pass through those doors of opportunity. Our chauffeur had opened that door himself when he asked, "So what kind of work do you people do?" He was very interested in my work as a psychic medium and quickly expressed his own belief system in the possibility that some people seem to have these amazing gifts even if the rest of us don't always understand how they work. This man was open and eager to hear the messages that came through to me for him from an angel.

You may be wondering what it is like to have a spirit connection with an angel so I will try to help you understand. Angels are spirits who, I believe, have achieved a higher level of spiritual growth whereby they attain angel status. The rank of becoming an angel within God's universe can only be achieved through hard work and strong, unrelenting faith and only our Higher Power determines "who" among us is an angel. Angels are spirits who are truly dedicated to assist the Universe, whom I call God, in every way possible and it appears to me that they have a sense of tenacity that keeps them focused on whatever mission that our Higher Power has guided them to complete. Some angels assist God from the other side, or heaven as it is often referred to, and others I have met are brought into Earthly lives to live a life path in which God guides them. Any angel living an Earthly life is not only here to help others but must also experience the challenges of any spiritual lessons or tests that the Universe provides within his or her life path.

Whenever I am given the opportunities to connect with an angel spirit I find that it feels almost as though another spirit being has got my back—is looking out for my best interests—and I welcome that kind of kinship energy. The methods of communication that I employ whenever I see, hear, feel, smell, or taste any kind of spirit message from an angel are the same as I explained to my readers in Chapter One of this book. All spirit connections are achieved via the transmission of spirit energy, which translates into spirit language between any and all of God's spirits in the universe, including angels, so I simply applied my psychic abilities to translate the messages from the angel who shared our limousine ride as I passed them on to our driver.

As we arrived at our hotel, the limousine driver unloaded our luggage and Bob paid him, along with a tip. Our driver smiled and repeatedly thanked me for doing my job to help him as a psychic medium. The messages that came through to me were very specific and personal to him. He felt they were very helpful as he had been wondering and worrying about some issues in his own life that he could not seem to find answers for on his own. I reminded him that God and angels are always around to help. Each of us needs only to choose to stay open to that process.

The limousine driver waved as he drove away leaving Bob and I to enter our hotel where we talked to the front desk clerk. It was still too early in the day for us to check into our room but we could check our luggage with the bell captain for now. That sounded great as we had left our home in Minnesota in the wee hours of the morning and just now realized that our appetites were large! Our first choice was to walk across the street to the beautiful green MGM Grand Las Vegas Hotel and Casino for a sumptuous buffet meal.

∞

I have been a fan of the "Wizard of Oz" movie for my entire life and the MGM Grand Las Vegas Hotel and Casino were designed in appearance, in such a way, that I felt as if Bob and I had finally arrived at the Emerald City. My own inner self gave me such a strong sense of positive energy that I felt a rush of energy from head to toe. Those gut instincts of mine were also pushing me to go forward into my own personal "Oz" experience. I was very excited, and I shared all that I was feeling with Bob, who was almost too hungry now to respond. We headed straight for the restaurant that served the buffet meal, and of course, we tried to make some decent food choices—but hey—we're not perfect. Bob and I smiled as we each filled our plates with some fruit, a few vegetables, and small servings of low-fat cottage cheese. Once seated at our table, we began laughing at our own choices because we had both topped our meals off with eggs, crepes, bacon, syrup, chicken, steak, and even a bite or two of yummy looking deserts! It's odd, but with our limited finances we couldn't help but notice that the buffet meal that we had been guided to was much more expensive than the buffets cost six years prior when we were in Las Vegas. That said, we both felt as though that meal might have been our one and only meal of the day, if we were to make our money last. *"Not to worry,"* was the thought that came swiftly from my intuition to my thinking mind. God had guided us here so I realized that we had to have strong faith. I understood that this whole trip required Bob and I to trust that everything we needed would come through the funds that we had. As always, I felt the guidance we needed would come to each of us in the perfect timing of the Universe.

Our appetites were finally sated, and our minds were feeling more able to focus as we exited the restaurant and took a moment to discuss where we each felt guided to go to next. I was feeling the strongest sense of intuition pulling me to a specific area of the casino. Bob also felt we should do some gaming, and he indicated that by turning towards me as he said, "Lead the way!" Within ten feet or so we came to a poker machine that both Bob and I felt a pull of energy towards. I really can't explain it any better than that. There was just a subtle sense of energy that drew me to that particular machine. No intuitive guidance came through to my thinking mind to tell me "This machine is a winner!" It was just another moment of intuition in my life when I am guided to pay close attention to how something *feels* to me in the sense of the energy. I should also note that I do not have any unfair advantage in gaming as a psychic medium because the Universe only allows each of us to win or lose exactly what we are meant to for the purpose of completing our individual spiritual lessons and tests. The sense of energy that I was feeling as I approached the poker machine was not unlike that which any person is capable of noticing. Many times a person will feel a sense to intuitively do something, including gaming, because the Universe, angels, and spirit guides have brought that person to that experience for his or her spiritual growth.

Bob seated himself at the poker slot machine while expressing the fact that he, too, felt drawn to play it and fairly quickly the machine hit a few small wins. This was a twenty-five cent slot machine and the twenty dollars that Bob had put into the machine had quickly worked its way up to a total of forty-five dollars. We both sensed that this was the most money that we were going to be paid on that particular machine so we agreed to cash out those meager winnings. Our motto was simple—we had to follow our gut instincts and have fun! We both know that there are times in gaming when a person wins a little bit; occasionally they may even win a larger jackpot. But most often, the money spent on gaming is simply the cost of the entertainment, nothing more and nothing less.

Next Bob moved to another slot machine that interested him, and I sat next to him as we took turns on the play. This is normally how we play any slot machine, in any casino, as it allows us to stay interactive with one another and to try to have fun as we play. Another big advantage of playing together on the same machine is that we are able to stay better focused on our own intuitive guidance so that when it is time to get off of any machine, we do. Gaming is never about spending hard earned money that you really should not be spending. In other words, never take your house payment, or your car payment, or your grocery money into a casino. Gaming should only be considered entertainment so only bring with you the amount of money that you can clearly afford to spend on leisure activities at that time in your life. That said, if the Universe guides you to a casino for some reason, my suggestion is to pay attention to that guidance and learn whatever it is that you need to experience from that situation or event.

It is my own experience that our Higher Power utilizes each and every opportunity in our life paths—even casinos and the concept of gaming—to test us as we also learn our individual spiritual lessons. Perhaps that revelation of mine may shock some of you, especially as it relates to the energy of addiction that can also be present within gaming opportunities. But the truth is, there is no way that a casino or any type of gaming establishment creates the energy of addiction. These are simply buildings with games that have no power or control over any one of us. In essence, they are neutral, meaning they are neither positive, nor negative in energy. These places, where the Universe guides many of us to experience spiritual lessons and tests through the process of gaming, are not to blame for any gambling addictions among humankind.

I can actually hear the gasps and feel the ground swell of judgment coming towards me for what I have just written. Stop here and remind yourself that I am not accepting of judgment from anyone, for any reason. And perhaps more important to note, is that each of us must always take responsibility for our own choices regarding anything we do in our lives. There is no way to dump our personal accountability onto someone or something else. As each of us pays closer attention to our own guidance from our Higher Power we will be made aware of the importance of personal accountability that I call karma.

Those among us who find themselves addicted to gaming are merely using "gambling" as the tool with which they bring controlled chaos into the lives of his or her loved ones, families, friends, acquaintances, and even total strangers. How is that accomplished? It is really quite simple; addicts chooses to gamble away the money that God has provided in their lives that is meant for food, clothing, and shelter—basic needs of humankind. When an addict no longer has the financial means to pay for those basic needs for themselves, their spouses, and their children, he or she will begin look to others to fill that need for money. As an addict looks to others for any source of financial means to help pay for their basic needs in life, they also begin to bring the energy of addiction into the lives of those persons whom the Universe has placed in the closest proximity. At the same time, controlled chaos is swiftly introduced, generally with a force of negativity and drama that leaves all persons feeling overwhelmed. The person who is addicted to gambling—or anything else for that matter—is counting on those responsible, thoughtful persons around them to be caught off guard. If the addict and their own energy of controlled chaos can keep us from focusing on our own moments of intuition, then it becomes easier for them to pressure us to enable them, to give them what they want.

Addicts find that there is no shortage of persons who are easy to manipulate, no matter what is it that the addict wants to take from them. There are so many people who are kind-hearted, generous, loving—and afraid or unwilling to stand up to the addicts in their lives and say "NO!" The generic term normally used to describe these persons who are so easily manipulated by addicts is *enabler*. We have all heard that word used to describe a person or persons who are often in the closest proximity to any addict that we know of. The enabler is the person or persons who have not yet learned enough about addiction and so the Universe will keep guiding them through their own life tests with the addicted persons closest to them.

So often these addicts are the very people we try the hardest to keep on loving but they push us hard until we question our sensibilities. They disrespect our life paths causing us to dig deeper to find that unconditional love that we have for them. Traditional methods and ideology about addiction offers so little real help that those of us who are responsible and sober often keep trying to help the addicts who surround us, in whatever ways we can think of. And as we say yes to any addict, the energy of controlled chaos grows stronger until it nearly suffocates our own positive energy.

Addiction is a choice within every spirit; enabling this energy to fill our lives with controlled chaos is also a choice that one's own inner self must make. And for me, the choice to quit enabling any person of addiction in my own life path came only after many years of tests through which God taught me about addictions of many kinds through my role as an enabler. One might wonder "why" the Universe would have guided my husband and I to a city, like Las Vegas, in which it is possible to feed the appetites of many who are addicted, but my gut instincts told me that we were protected from the negative energy of addiction and that we simply needed to trust in our Higher Power who would reveal all of the positive spiritual lessons and tests that were meant to be experienced in the city that never sleeps. Our trip to Las Vegas, Nevada in July 2005 had actually felt quite positive thus far and, since I was unwilling to allow any sense of addiction energy to block my life path, it felt only right to continue to live in the moments of our combined intuition.

As Bob and I moved around in the MGM Grand Las Vegas casino I continued to feel such a positive sense within me and I was trying to stay in that "Emerald City" energy. I can only relate it to the sense that we see in the "Wizard of Oz" movie when Dorothy and her friends have finally arrived at a place where they feel that only good things can happen for them. Like Dorothy and her pals, both Bob and I have worked so hard to heal since my son, Brady, died on December 31, 2000 from his own choice of suicide. The healing process had left little time, energy, or finances for anything else.

I allowed myself to wander freely about the casino, always aware of the subtle current of energy guiding me.

That is hard to explain—this "energy" that I speak of—except to me it is quite normal and something that I have learned will never lie or deceive me no matter the situation or location that I find myself in.

The energy of the Universe is there for each of us to pick up on if only we choose to become aware of it. Without really having to try anymore, I have discovered that I am able to sense positive and negative energies in any person, place, or thing. This does not depend upon distance, as there is no limitation to this energy. It can be felt anywhere, at any time.

In July 2005, as I moved freely around in that casino, I felt the energy pull of something positive in my path at that moment. Bob followed closely, and we chatted along the way.

Suddenly I felt like I should stop and play a one dollar machine that was connected to a group of machines, all promising a chance at a progressively growing jackpot. I faced the machine that I personally felt intuitively guided to play and saw that the maximum credits required to play for a chance to win the progressive jackpot was two dollars. I was also very aware that this is *not* the type of slot machine that I normally like to play as it is the typical "777" style where all three reels must line up to win. To be honest, I find these machines rather boring, but that was where my intuition had guided me and I trusted that my Higher Power had a reason for this.

Bob handed me a twenty-dollar bill to begin playing my choice in machines, then he took a step back from me, just watching. He was perplexed by my choice to play that machine, and he quickly observed the other machines in the row. Bob realized that several other machines that were linked into this group progressive slot program offered higher dollar amounts if a person should win the jackpot on any of those particular machines. My husband relayed this information to me as I continued to hit the button marked "play max credits" on my chosen machine.

To be quite candid, the machine I was guided to play was not much fun to start with. My original investment of twenty dollars was gone within minutes, and my husband looked dismayed when I ask him for another twenty dollar bill to feed that machine. Bob said, "Okay, but I'm telling you, the odds of winning on that machine don't look too good!"

I love my husband dearly, and I respect his viewpoint on all matters. However, both he and I know that I will always stay true to my own moments of intuition because that is the way in which the Universe is guiding me, for whatever reasons known or unknown to me at that time. And so I continued to sit quietly in front of the slot machine that my Higher Power had guided me to play. I nodded my head to acknowledge that I heard my husband's words, while at the same time holding out my hand to receive the twenty dollars from Bob that I felt I was guided to add to that machine.

In spite of Bob's doubts about that machine, in spite of the fact that the machine hadn't hit much yet, I stayed positive. Most importantly, I stayed true to my own personal guidance as it made its way through my own strong intuition.

Bob started to wander away, but after just two more spins on that machine, I said to him, "You might want to rethink your theory about my odds on this machine!" My husband turned back to face me with a puzzled look in his eyes. I lifted my hand towards my machine and Bob saw that the "777" symbols all lined up. The word "JACKPOT" illuminated the screen on my machine as the noisy music began to play.

As the casino attendant arrived to pay me my jackpot winnings of $1,026.89 I was aware of God's voice in my head. *"I will always provide whatever you need, as you need it. Just follow where I guide you and everything will be revealed in its own sense of timing."*

Right about now I sense my readers all wondering if this is the way it is for a psychically gifted person when he or she tries their luck at any sort of gaming. In other words, you are wondering if Bob and I are always winners. The answer is a simple no. We have found that whenever we have been guided to do any gaming there is always the clear sense that we will learn something from that time spent. Quite often, we find that most machines will pay very small wins that allow a person to continue gaming *if only* you pay attention to your gut instincts and get off of any machine when you are guided through your own intuition to do so. Occasionally, I do feel a very strong pull of energy towards a machine, and yes, quite often that proves to be a very positive experience for me. That may even mean a somewhat larger win of money—*but only if God allows that to be*! In other words, the Universe will only give each of us exactly the amount of money that we need in our life paths at any given time. Each of us will only have access to the exact amount of money that is required to learn our own spiritual lessons and tests in any given moment. No more and no less is ever needed; therefore no more and no less is ever provided. Think of it this way: in spite of my own strong psychic abilities and my own strong intuition, I will only win at some form of gaming if that is the means by which my Higher Power is choosing to get that amount of monies into my hands. Additionally, if it is not time in my own life path for me to have greater financial means provided by the Universe, then I will not have it by any means. The exact same concepts apply to each and every person who may be intuitively guided to do some form of gaming along his or her life path. Each of us will only win when it is time for us to have that experience. Each of us will lose when it is time for us to have *that* experience.

A psychic medium is like any other person who wins; sometimes it is our turn to win and other times we simply feed the machine for the next person's opportunity, as well as for our own life lessons. And as I stood beside that winning machine in the MGM Grand Las Vegas casino, I knew that the jackpot that the Universe just placed into my hands was meant to be seed money for the working vacation that God had sent us on. Clearly God felt that we needed those winnings to move forward along our respective paths as we each navigated our way through Las Vegas. Bob and I both breathed a sigh of relief, and were happy that I had paid attention to my own moments of intuition. Now it was time to step out of this "Oz" adventure and to explore more of beautiful Las Vegas, Nevada!

∞

We decided it was time to venture out into the desert heat of Las Vegas, Nevada and to stretch our legs as we walked down the sidewalks, always mindful of which direction God was guiding us. Although Bob and I had only been in that city for a couple of hours we were already experiencing the strongest sense of intuitive guidance that was clearly going to keep us moving along at a steady pace. We had no idea exactly "why" God had brought us here, other than my own sense that there was psychic work to be done. As is always the case, I knew that psychic work would continue to be revealed to me in whatever ways it was needed.

The rest of that first day was spent checking into our hotel, as well as walking to and from various casinos and other hotels. The heat was awe-inspiring and I learned quickly that it was best if I carried a bottle of water with me anytime we walked outside. The mere action of walking a block or two, in that heat, left us parched and dry. It was a simple choice to carry water along with us, and one that certainly felt right to me, as there was no desire on my part to have another episode of heat stroke like I did in New York City back in the hot summer of 1988.

I mention the heat of that desert city, not only because it was the hottest I have ever dealt with in my lifetime—temperatures between 110 to 116 degrees Fahrenheit—but there is also the importance of respecting the energy of any place, of any situation that the Universe guides us into. It is my own belief system that each of us can choose to be safe and protected by the very positive energy of our Higher Power no matter where our path takes us, but that protection must be accompanied by full respect for any guidance that we receive through our own intuition. In other words, I already knew that I do not personally do well in high levels of heat from my own past experience. To be honest, I knew that I could easily go into a state of being that could cause my physical body to shut down, to die.

Extreme heat is that tough on me. My family physician reiterated that to me, in no uncertain terms, after the severe heat stroke and dehydration that I suffered in August 1988. However, it was now July 2005 and my own intuition and guidance were clear. There was no doubt in my mind that God wanted me to be in Las Vegas for reasons that would be revealed only when it was time. I had to let go of my own fears about walking outdoors in the heat. I had to trust that my body, mind, and spirit were all encompassed with the utmost protection from my Higher Power. It was obvious and apparent to me that there was no way that God was going to let me just stay in the air-conditioned comfort of our hotel room. Somewhere out on the streets of Las Vegas, Nevada, and in the various casinos and other establishments, were the very people that God was guiding me to meet so that I could pass on some psychic messages that were needed. This required me to let go of my own discomfort and to keep moving along this well-lit portion of my own life path that happened to be in glittering Las Vegas.

It didn't take long for me to find more of the psychic work that I was brought here to do. The very next morning Bob and I chose to eat a breakfast buffet at the Excalibur hotel and casino that was about three blocks away from our hotel. Once again, there was to be no taxi or shuttle for us, as we were each guided through our intuition to "keep walking."

∞

The Excalibur hotel and casino is another one of the more famous themed hotels and casinos that draws its patrons in through the use of fantasy surroundings and images. The Excalibur theme is one that is based upon knights in shining armor in a castle type of environment. Within the context of that theme, the casino still catered to all of the traditional gaming choices that most patrons seek out. And just like in most modern day casinos, a person can look in almost any direction while at Excalibur, and see slot machines and table games of nearly every possible denomination. Black jack, craps, keno, roulette and various kinds of poker give even the most cautious player a chance to win—or to lose. Again, keep in mind that each of us will always win or lose exactly what God guides us to, within the context of our own spiritual lessons and tests. That is something that my own intuitive guidance from the Universe has taught me firmly, with no exceptions.

On that particular morning we were not yet being guided to participate in any of the gaming. In its place, after eating our fill at yet another wonderful breakfast buffet, Bob and I decided to look through some of the shops located within the Excalibur complex. Here is where I felt my own intuition leading me into a shop full of statues and souvenirs. As I moved towards the door of the gift shop, Bob suddenly decided that he wanted to look at another shop and so we split up, each going in the direction that he or she felt was right for them.

I entered the shop of my choice and was immediately drawn to an area where there were some lovely statues. My gaze immediately fell upon a rather unusual statue of an angel. The female figurine looked quite different that most angel statues as she was built more thinly. There was a beautiful energy of humility emanating from the statue; I felt that she was meant to be mine. I looked closely at that angelic statue and yet, as much as I wanted to purchase it and take it back home to Minnesota with me, my own common sense started to take hold.

The angel was about twelve inches high, with very detailed wings that spread out horizontally, to a width of about twelve inches as well. She was made of some sort of heavy rosin material, but it was also clear to me that she was extremely fragile. I looked closely at her and my mind was full of doubt. I could see no way in which she could be transported safely back to my home in Minnesota. Her wings were so delicate and breakable that it was more than likely that she would arrive at my home in a damaged condition after my airline flight. I sighed. It isn't often that I find something that really connects with me in this way, but I had to be sensible, didn't I?

As I walked away from "my angel" I noticed that there was a sign indicating that items on another shelf were on sale for a whopping 75% discount. By the very placement of the sign, the sale price did not seem to include my angel.

Suddenly the employee of the shop began to speak to me, just making small talk. I looked up and saw a woman in her early sixties, and I heard a thick accent when she spoke. I did not recognize her accent and found that I had to focus intently on her words in order to understand her. As I listened closely, I realized that she had noticed my interest in the angel figurine and was now asking if she could "Wrap that up?" for me. My head shook no as I approached the sales counter. I tried to bridge the gap of our two different languages by explaining my concerns about getting the statue home on the airplane without breaking it.

The sales woman was pleasant and insisted that she could wrap it in so much bubble wrap that it would not be damaged. I told her that the small angelic sculpture cost $64.00 and that was too much money for me to spend on something that was so fragile. She smiled broadly and pointed to the 75% off sale sign. In her broken English, the sales lady kindly explained that my cost would only be $16.00! We both smiled and I knew that God was trying hard to get me that beautiful angel statue for my home. Now I could only nod yes, and took out my wallet to pay for the item while she wrapped it up with love—and lots of bubble wrap!

There was no one else in that gift shop except for the kindhearted sales woman and myself yet I suddenly felt the presence of an older female spirit. The spirit quickly spoke to me (psychically) and introduced herself as the mother of the sales woman. I heard the spirit's voice as thoughts in my head. The elderly mother had died nearly a year before, but still her daughter was in deep grief. The spirit asked me to pass on a few messages to her daughter, and I was also guided by God, in those moments, to oblige.

These two women, elderly mother and daughter, had been quite close during their lives, and the message was coming clearly that this daughter needed to "let go of her own guilt" over her mother's death. The mother's spirit explained that her daughter was wracked with guilt because she could not keep her mother alive as she suffered through a painful and terminal illness. The mother's spirit wanted her daughter to know that she was "no longer in pain and with my Lord and Savior Jesus Christ." The mother's spirit had lived her own life as God had intended, and now she wanted her daughter to move out of the painful energy of grief and to heal. This was necessary for the daughter to be able to move forward, and to fully experience her own life path, for the remainder of her time here on Earth.

God was guiding me to explain to the sales clerk that I was a psychic medium. In response to that news, the sales clerk told me she was from a country in Europe that held a strong belief system in psychic abilities. She expressed to me that she would like very much to hear any of the messages that were coming through my psychic abilities that were meant for her.

For the next several minutes I worked hard to communicate the messages that were coming through to me from her elderly mother's spirit. There were many specific details provided by her mother's spirit that the sales woman verified immediately. We had never before met, and I found that we both had to be willing to speak clearly, and to listen closely, because of our language differences. However, as my psychic work progressed, there was no doubt left in either of our minds that God had guided me into her shop that morning for more than just the purchase of an angel.

Soon the psychic messages were completed, and the sales woman I had just met thanked me profusely as she handed me my carefully wrapped angel figurine. That whole incident took only about forty minutes of my morning, and I did not charge the woman for my psychic work as God had guided me to do that particular bit of psychic work at "no charge."

Beyond all that had just transpired in that Las Vegas gift shop I have already learned that the measure of my own psychic gifts will always be determined by my Higher

Power, and often in those moments of intuition as he guides me to use my gifts. I have become fully and completely aware, through the course of my work, that these amazing psychic gifts that God gave me are priceless.

And although God does guide me to use my psychic abilities and my spiritual knowledge to help others, occasionally at "no charge", I am still living a life here on Earth that requires money to pay the bills. Just as the way in which I am generally guided to do my work is quite unique, I find that my own paychecks seem to come through God in rather unusual ways, like the early win on the slot machine the day before. But all of this is just another way in which my life path requires me to stand strong in my faith as I never know when or where I will receive another of God's surprise "paychecks" to me!

In those moments in the gift shop, I felt such a wonderful sense of awe and appreciation for the way in which God had brought the sales woman and I together, just as the day had begun. That encounter with spirit had left us both feeling so connected to one another, and to the energy of our Higher Power. Our language differences could not stop the messages from the spirit of a loved one that was meant to help heal. There was nothing left to do but smile and wave as I left the store and joined Bob, who had found himself a comfortable bench to sit upon while powerful moments of intuition and spirit connections were taking place mere steps away.

∞

Our working vacation continued with more hot weather, more great food, and more gaming. Here and there, in various casinos, we found ourselves guided by the Universe to different types of slot machines and table games. At times we were given the opportunity to win various amounts of money; other times we lost our meager gaming funds with little or no fanfare. In one casino we learned how to play roulette, and found that our money appeared to last only as long as it needed to. As soon as the dealers changed on that particular roulette table, God guided a psychic message through me to pass on to the new dealer. Like most people I meet, that man was also very open to receiving his messages that were coming to me psychically, and all was done within a couple of minutes. Just as quickly as my psychic work was completed with him, Bob and I placed our last bets on the roulette table and lost with a spin of the wheel. The timing of this was not lost on either of us! My husband and I left the roulette table smiling and contented. We had learned a new game, and another person was given their psychic messages. It was very easy for the two of us to stay relaxed as we followed the flow of our own moments of intuition. Early in our trip we recognized the fact that we had to trust that all would be provided. In doing so, we saw that the funding had already been provided by God just by following our intuition during our brief stay in Las Vegas.

On the third afternoon in the city of lights, Bob and I found ourselves wandering around in a section of the casino and hotel known as New York New York. As the name implies, that themed casino and hotel derives its look and theme from New York City. Everywhere we turned there were sights and sounds, as well as the aroma of great foods, that allowed a person to experience the best of New York in a casino environment. My own connection to energy is amazingly strong and I found that this casino really did bring forth the similarity to the hustle and bustle of New York City's energy on a busy day.

Tired of walking, my husband, Bob, and I decided to seat ourselves on the first (and only) available bench within an open mall area that was surrounded by small vendors and shops. I personally felt a strong sense that we needed to do some "people watching" in that area, but was not yet sure why that was required of us by the Universe. It was about one o'clock in the afternoon, and with the smell of New York hot dogs wafting through the air, Bob and I decided to share a hot dog and a cold glass of lemonade.

After about twenty minutes of loitering on the bench, Bob was getting restless. Still, I felt something was happening that was going to need my attention. I explained to Bob that I really felt a strong pull to my right—actually to a nearby ice cream store. Bob laughed and said, "Robin, if you want ice cream just say so!"

My own intuitive sense was coming stronger, even as he spoke those words, and so I stood up and began walking towards the ice cream shop. There were only four or five other patrons in the store at that time and a small table for two beckoned us. We quickly seated ourselves; both of us sat facing the direction of the sales counter. I was sitting in the chair nearest to the large open doorway that connected the shop to the open mall area.

Our decision to have an ice cream cone was made without hesitation and Bob walked over to the counter to place our order with the teenage girl on duty. My entire focus was now on the energy I was feeling in that shop as something was amiss. Before long my psychic abilities came alive and my eyesight followed the path of the energy that had led me here.

Ah, yes! There it was—practically jumping out at me—a large purse draped over the back of a chair with its owner nowhere in sight! I jumped up and moved quickly over to rescue that purse before someone could steal it. A full purse sitting by itself anywhere is an open invitation to even the most bungling of thieves, but here in this city of wins and losses, the Universe surely knew that it wouldn't be long before the contents of that purse would be stolen and the owner would be left reeling with the ramifications of that loss. How do I know? That's an easy one. It's because I, too, have experienced my own purse and identity being stolen many years prior. That is not something that I would want anyone else to go through, not if I can help in any way. So the fact that God could, and did, guide me to that location to help the owner of that forgotten purse made a great deal of sense to me.

The purse was quite heavy as I carried it up to the sales counter in the ice cream store, as I felt guided to do. Bob was just getting our ice cream cones when I explained the situation to the young store employee. I was firm and very clear with her that the owner would be coming back for the purse, but that she needed to confirm the description of the missing purse *before* giving it back. This was all coming strongly to me through my own psychic senses, and I trust all that God gives me through these gifts. The young woman employee agreed to take possession of the purse and tucked it safely underneath the back of the counter. I then sat back down in my chair at the small table with Bob to enjoy our ice cream cones.

In less than five minutes, a woman in her late fifties ran into the ice cream store and became hysterical. She was screaming and pointing to where she had last left her purse. Before anyone could speak, that very upset woman ran back out into the open mall area. I ran after her as she weaved and dodged her way through the crowd. Soon I saw that she had just run back to be with her elderly mother, who appeared to be having some sort of health crisis as there were authorities gathered around her to help.

The woman who had forgotten her purse in the ice cream shop certainly had her hands full, and I quickly calmed her as I explained that her purse was safe and unharmed. Together we walked back to the ice cream store so that she could claim her purse. That poor woman was so thankful that I had stepped up to place her purse in safekeeping, but she was also struck deeply by a feeling of disbelief. I felt great empathy for this complete stranger as I saw that she was visibly shaking from all that was happening to her that afternoon. In her own hurry to get her elderly mother some assistance, the woman had simply walked away from her own purse and its contents.

She shared with me the fact that all of her cash, her credit cards, and her airplane ticket were in that purse. All of her identification was in that very important, but nondescript purse of hers. We both knew that a thief could have easily grabbed that purse and disappeared into the crowds of Las Vegas never to be seen again. The look of gratitude on her face was enough for me. I knew that God had simply asked me to step up and help another person—that woman, a total stranger—who was already going to be stressed today by the health concerns of her own ailing mother. It was evident to me that the woman's own path did not need to include having her purse stolen on that July afternoon. However, it was also apparent to me that this woman was not someone who felt comfortable reaching out to help a total stranger herself. I believe that God guided me to help her because there will be a time coming soon in her own life path when the Universe will push her beyond her own comfort zone to reach out and help a total stranger. In order to do that, this woman needed to have this rather traumatic event unfold in her own path so that she could draw upon that at a later time.

As is always the case, my intuition guided me there to help. But in that situation, my own psychic abilities were also used to put whatever steps I needed to take into action. And just as quickly as all of these events fell into place, it was now over, and time for Bob and I to enjoy more of our vacation.

∞

With any vacation time spent in Las Vegas, Nevada there is almost an unspoken obligation that it must include a person's own choice in musical entertainment. This busy city has another nickname and that is "the entertainment capital of the world!" So once again, I followed the steady and clear guidance that was coming through my own moments of intuition and that led us on another walk outdoors to a place that sold discounted show tickets. We really had no preconceived thoughts about whom we might want to see perform on a Las Vegas stage, so both Bob and I stayed open to all possibilities. That whole working vacation had, so far, been quite interesting and rewarding, and we discovered many years ago that living in the moments of our intuition feels right to both of us.

There was no delay in recognizing which tickets we were being guided by the Universe to purchase that day. Wayne Newton was an entertainment legend and by all standards, a Las Vegas "must see." That was the name and the image of the face that kept coming into both of our thinking minds simultaneously as Bob and I stood in line to purchase show tickets. We felt in harmony with this intuitive guidance and so we made our purchase for Wayne Newton's performance at nine o'clock that same evening. Included in the ticket purchase was the name of another entertainer who was listed as the opening act for Wayne Newton. Bob asked me if I knew anything about the other entertainer but I couldn't share anything with him, as I had never heard of that person before. All I knew was that the performances we would be attending were being held at the Las Vegas Hilton Hotel and Casino.

Late in the afternoon we rode the Las Vegas monorail system from the MGM Grand Las Vegas Hotel and Casino platform entrance all the way to the Las Vegas Hilton Hotel and Casino. The distance between those two locations was far too great for us to walk safely in that extreme heat so it was a welcome relief to use the monorail transportation system. Our vacation time thus far had been spent exploring the many opportunities at one end of the Las Vegas strip. Bob and I were both looking forward to whatever that afternoon would bring us as we exited the monorail platform by the Las Vegas Hilton, located several blocks from our hotel.

When I entered the Las Vegas Hilton Hotel and Casino I was immediately struck by the energy within. I have already made mention of my own strong relationship with energy as it is the ultimate tool of communication for any psychically gifted person. Every person, every place, and every thing are all made of energy. This energy is not visible to the naked eye, and yet it is unmistakable to someone like me—a truly gifted psychic who can feel positive energy, negative energy, as well as the energy of every single emotion. What most people do not realize is that *every one of us*—the "every person" who is a reader of my books—can also feel energy if only they choose to.

The energy of the Las Vegas Hilton Hotel and Casino was overwhelmingly positive and uplifting. I had already been in and out of many other buildings and locations in Las Vegas, and found it to be similar to most other cities. Every town and city has areas that feel quite positive, as well as they all have some locations that feel quite negative in energy. My own experiences in Las Vegas had already allowed me to feel that same flow and variation in energy as Bob and I had walked from place to place.

I have learned that energy not only varies from location to location, but it is also important to understand that the energy can be quite different within the same room of any location. In other words, a room or building can feel quite positive in its energy, but then very quickly I can feel negative energy moving into that room, or it may occupy just a small space of that room.

Within the Las Vegas Hilton Hotel and Casino my own gaze lifted to the high ceilings as I viewed one sparkling crystal chandelier after another. The light was radiant as it bounced from fine cut crystal to crystal. I stopped walking to close my eyes and just allowed myself to take in the positive energy. My husband knows that I have always been attracted to crystals as each kind has a distinct energy of its own. Again, it is hard to describe what that feels like except to say that the energy of crystals feels quite positive to my inner self. In many cultures there is a belief system that various crystals contain healing energies to assist our spirits. All I know is that I can personally feel the energy in crystals, and most often that feels positive to my spirit.

As I have already mentioned, most of the newer casinos and hotels in Las Vegas are theme based. The one I was standing in was exceptional to me as it felt like a classy homage to days gone by. There were references to Elvis Presley, the legendary entertainer, as Bob and I promptly learned that this was the place where Elvis broke attendance records for his Las Vegas shows. The energy composition of today mixed easily there with the spirits of the past. Yes, I could already sense that I was going to enjoy our time spent at the Las Vegas Hilton Hotel and Casino!

There was some time before dinner so Bob and I decided to play some blackjack at the gaming tables. We met some fun people at various tables that we played on, but we also observed a woman who was in way too deep. By that I mean that it was painfully obvious to us, and to all who shared that blackjack table, that this middle-aged woman was addicted to gaming. She spent the entire time playing blackjack from such a high level of anxiety and stress that she never enjoyed the process. Her bets swung wildly from very high to very low, and back again. She constantly changed from playing just one hand in front of her, to playing two hands of blackjack, always trying hard to win back her losses. I watched her eyes—the windows to our own inner self—and saw that she was in deep despair over her continued losses. And yet, this woman would not walk away. There was the unmistakable energy of helplessness that came from her inner self, as if to say, "I'm not responsible for what I do here because I am an addict."

Gaming and those who have been addicted to it, as well as those who profit from the gaming losses of others, are two areas where the Universe has given me a front row seat. My own observations of the woman at the blackjack table left me with the strong sense that "Yes, ma'am, you absolutely ARE responsible for your choices *no matter what*" but I was not guided to engage in any discussion with the woman or to share my observations.

Soon the entire table emptied itself, one by one, as each of the other blackjack players follow their own gut instincts to stop playing with that woman. As I have already stated, gaming should be considered a form of entertainment and should not be viewed as a place to spend monies that are required for your basic living needs.

∞

The events of our day had caused us to work up an appetite and our choice was to continue sampling what was advertised as another one of "the finest buffets" in the city of lights. Dinner tonight for Bob and I would be in the buffet restaurant of the Las Vegas Hilton. The theme of understated elegance continued into the restaurant and we found ourselves thoroughly enjoying our meal that night. In my own private ranking system, I told Bob, "This buffet gets my vote so far for the best in Las Vegas." The food choices were all seasoned so delicately so that nothing became overbearing. And yet within that buffet setting there was an abundance of opportunities to sample nearly any cuisine that a palate could desire. The word "classy" comes to mind even as I write about this past experience.

After dinner we walked around inside the hotel and casino structures to stretch our legs in air-conditioned comfort before it was time to be seated in the theatre for Wayne Newton's performance. We had no discussion about the opening act performer and really no prior expectations about whether or not we would enjoy that part of tonight's show.

Finally we took our pre-assigned seats as indicated by our tickets. Bob and I occupied seats 62 and 63 in row N of section M-3 that placed us on the far left, rear as we faced the performing stage. Bob joked with me that he wondered why God didn't get us front row seats if we were supposed to be here tonight. I giggled as I scoped out the view and the vantage point that we had been placed in for that night's entertainment. It felt to me as though our assigned seats would be perfect—and in hindsight, they were. Soon we fell quiet and became mesmerized by the singing performance of the young man who had the job of warming up the audience in preparation for the headliner, Wayne Newton.

The opening act was a man who appeared to be in his 20's but his spirit certainly felt to me to be that of an old soul. His music and his voice touched me deep in the heart of my inner self, my spirit. Bob and I shared a look between us that said, "WOW!" I also said a silent, "Thank you" to the Universe for guiding us here to be a part of that experience. In all parts of me—spirit, mind, and body—I was made completely and fully aware by the Universe, by God, that this young man was a person whose own life journey had been full of challenges and yet, his life plan was to help many others in their own journeys of healing. How could he do that? Simply by following his own intuitive guidance from God and using the amazing gift he was given—his own voice. How did I know that as I listened to his singing performance? God's voice filled my head with much psychic information about that young man. I understood, in those moments, that this relatively unknown singer was the reason Bob and I were guided there on that night.

As the young man completed his singing performance, there was no doubt in that audience's collective mind that he had done his job quite well! The entire audience seemed to be totally "warmed up" and ready to enjoy the music of the headliner, Wayne Newton. The energy was positive and electrifying. I could have personally kept listening to that new performer sing for hours.

In a standing ovation, the young man left the stage and Wayne Newton entered. Of course, there was thunderous applause to greet the long-standing Las Vegas landmark and performer. Everyone seemed happy to have the chance to hear Wayne Newton sing as well.

Somewhere during that night's performances, the audience was given the information that the young man who had opened the show for Mr. Newton had been the winner of a televised contest earlier that year. As a part of that contest, the young singer had been awarded the opportunity to work in Las Vegas, Nevada as the opening act for Wayne Newton himself. As I sat listening to Wayne Newton discussing the many opportunities that the young man had won as a result of performing well in that contest it was obvious to me that, by anyone's standards, that young man certainly had been given special blessings by the Universe.

When Wayne Newton finished his performance that night I had acquired a full sense of appreciation for his talent as well. Again, I am grateful that God guided us there on that night to see his show in the venue that has served Mr. Newton so well for years now. He truly embodies the title of "Mr. Las Vegas" in his bigger than life singing concert.

After the show Bob and I exited the theatre along with all of the other patrons. I was guided intuitively by our Higher Power to *"stay in the area near the theatre doors that we just exited,"* and so we did, just waiting for God's guidance as Bob and I stood about ten feet or so from the interior doors of the theatre. Bob began to get antsy and wanted to go do something, but I asked him to be patient. I did not know "who" would be coming to that location, but God was giving me the strongest sense that I needed to do some psychic work right now. A few minutes later, I saw that the young male singer had arrived and was standing by the theatre doors, ready to sign autographs for his new fans. There was no doubt in my mind that *he* was meant to receive some psychic messages at that time.

I waited patiently for the young performer to speak to his waiting fans, and it was a joy to connect with his exuberant and positive energy. Finally there was no one left, and I approached this very talented young man. I introduced myself and explained the psychic work that I do. The young man was immediately open and receptive to my work, and told me that he was humbled to be getting messages through me at that time. His words rang true to my inner self and so I paid close attention to the guidance that God was giving me at that time.

As I said earlier in this chapter, this was not a person that I knew anything about but that does not ever affect the psychic work that I do or the messages that the Universe asks me to pass on. It is never necessary for me to have prior knowledge of any person or his or her life events in order to do my job as a gifted psychic medium. All that was required of me in those moments was to listen, to watch, and to feel all of the different messages that God was asking me to pass on to the young man who had just entertained us.

There were specific details that came to me psychically that this young man verified immediately. There was the energy of a strong female spirit that felt to me as though she had been a "mothering energy" to him, but she quickly identified herself as "the grandmother". As I told the young man about this his eyes widened, and then they filled with love. At that moment the amazing singer spoke of his own close connection to his grandmother who was a powerful force in his young life.

As the psychic messages continued, I told the young man that God had some pretty positive things to say about him, his voice, and his future. But there were also some things about the hardships in his life that had brought him to that place in time that were powerfully significant in shaping him, preparing him if you will, for the road that lie ahead. And perhaps the most important message that I was asked to pass on to this young man, a virtual stranger to me, was that *it was very important that this young man continue to follow his own strong intuition—his own gut instincts—no matter "how" anyone else thought he should do things.* The comparison was shown to me that, although Wayne Newton was helping God at that time to mentor this budding star in his new career, when all was said and done, their two musical career paths would not be at all similar.

The musical career path of the young man would be like no other, and in saying that God reiterated to me that, *"This young man must follow closely in his own unique path."* That message was strong and came through very forcefully as I explained to the young adult singer that his background and his music were so healing to draw upon and that he should never look upon his past experiences as "negative". All of what he had gone through were meant to be a positive learning experience and were what was now feeding his inspirational singing spirit within.

When the psychic messages were completed, the young man thanked me and gave me a warm hug. We both felt the energy of our Higher Power surrounding us in those moments of intuition and God left me with the clear sense that it had been very important that I pay close attention to my intuition and there was no doubt in my mind that, for some reason unknown to me, this young man needed to get those messages from his grandmother's spirit and from our Higher Power as they were brought through my psychic gifts. I also knew that the true meaning of those messages would be put to the test as the young man moved forward in his chosen life path. The perception that he has of his own successes or failures are entirely up to him as well as it is up to him to pay attention to God, angels, and spirit guides as they try to assist him from time-to-time.

In writing this chapter of my book, I was strongly guided to share part of the messages that God asked me to pass on to that young entertainer because they also apply to me, and to so many of you, my readers. The very message that so many of us have painful pasts that could leave us overflowing with negativity—if we choose to perceive it that way—is a powerful one. Those lessons and tests in our past were always meant to teach us and to help us grow spiritually—if only we choose to accept all of it as a positive piece of inspiration for our own futures. And once again God showed me that no person is truly a stranger to another. We must always be open to meeting and sharing our gifts when it is time in the Universe. Whenever that happens, it will always feel right to everyone involved.

Now, you may wonder, "Why does Robin do it? Why does she go up to total strangers to pass on these messages from God, from angels, and from the spirits of our loved ones?" The answer is obvious and clear to my spirit, mind, and body: This is who I am, and this is what I was brought into this life to do. There is nothing more fulfilling or more important for me to spend my life on. Everything in my past has prepared me for these moments of intuition as they unfold. All that has been required of me is acceptance. Acceptance of me as the very being that God wants me to be . . . acceptance of these amazing psychic gifts that God has blessed me with . . . and finally, acceptance that all I have to do is my part and God will take care of the rest of his Universe as needed.

∞

Perhaps you are thinking that this is where my chapter ends, but not so fast! There are occasions in my own life path where even I am surprised at how quickly one situation flows into another. As I walked away from my psychic work with that young man I was feeling the most comforting and positive energy surrounding me. There were many angels around Bob and I as we walked from the theatre out towards the casino. I am always able to see any angel or spirit that God allows me to see with my psychic abilities. There is no way for me to stop this nor can I somehow cause it to happen. Whatever the Universe allows to be experienced is what a person will be a part of. And besides, the reward of "seeing, feeling, and getting to talk to angels or spirits" is one of life's wonderful occurrences that I am aware of from time-to-time, and one that I never tire of.

We walked a short distance and then entered the casino as Bob held my hand and leaned over to say, "I'm proud of you, honey!" I appreciate all of the support and positive energy that I can get in my work as it has many challenges of its own. But before I could say that, I was suddenly having a connection with another spirit who was now right in front of me. The spirit was that of a man, who quickly identified himself to me and said, "Hi Robin, follow me!" Instantly God guided me to pay attention to that man's spirit and to follow my own intuition through what would transpire.

I quickly told Bob that I needed to do something and he followed me as I turned towards my left and took a couple of steps down into a High Stakes area of the casino. This wasn't a really large area but it had some slot machines that required a player to bet larger amounts as they played. Bob shot me a look of confusion. He quickly spoke up and said, "Robin, this is probably a little too rich for our budget, don't you think?"

Normally I would agree, but this was just one of those times when I knew that I needed to pay attention to whatever the Universe was giving me in my own separate guidance. I asked Bob if he could also see the spirit of the man who was walking—well, actually "floating"—just in front of me. Bob has strong psychic gifts as well but he doesn't use them in the same way that I do. My husband replied, "No, I don't see anything or anyone."

I followed the spirit to a specific slot machine that allowed a person to bet on hands of poker. God guided me to *"sit down and play"* and so I did. Before I put any money into the slot machine, I felt it was time to tell Bob about the spirit that had guided me there. The spirit of Elvis Presley—singer, actor, and legendary entertainer—had shown himself to me in what I would describe as a hologram form that I could "see" with my physical eyes. Elvis Presley's spirit appeared in front of me and spoke to me clearly in those brief moments since entering the casino. Yes, it was Elvis Presley's spirit that God had asked to bring me to the particular slot machine in the High Stakes area.

It is not unusual for the spirit of a famous or well-known person to communicate psychically with me from time-to-time. That occurs whenever God allows it, and while I have great respect for these "celebrity spirits", I also treat them with the same level of interest and respect that I would if your grandmother's spirit connected with me. In other words, we are all equally important as the very spirits that we are.

That said, I was intrigued to find out "why" God had enlisted the spirit of Elvis to bring me to that particular slot machine immediately after my psychic work with the young male singer had been completed. I felt strongly that it was time to put some money into that machine and take this adventure to the next level! Bob was still in a very cautious mode of energy as he handed me a $100 bill from his wallet. We both had the sense of intuition that I was to play that machine by myself for some reason so I began by playing just one credit . . . then another . . . which led me to continue to follow my guidance to slowly increase the number of credits as the machine hit a few credits here and there.

In less than a minute, all of the money was gone. It was only at that time that I became aware that this was a $25 slot machine. That means that every single credit played would cost the player $25! With that new piece of information brought to my attention, I turned to Bob and requested another $100 bill to continue playing the machine that God and Elvis' spirit had brought me to. My husband turned a weird shade of pale white as he asked me "Are you *sure*?"

The only response that I could give Bob was the one that I stay true to in my life— **no matter what**. I told my husband that I had to follow my own intuition that had brought me here and that God was still guiding me strongly. I had no idea what this whole event was about, other than I had to trust this experience as something that I was meant to have. That said, I inserted the second $100 bill and resumed playing poker on the slot machine. Two more turns on the machine and I finally won a few credits, which to be honest, made both Bob and I breathe a collective sigh of relief. My own guidance was now so strong that I could feel God's energy, and I could see Elvis Presley's spirit hovering right over the machine. I looked at

Bob and hit the "play" button on the machine again. In an instant there were four kings on the screen of that machine indicating a win of over $600! I smiled at my husband, and then I looked up at the friendly spirit of Elvis as I saw him break into a huge grin! With that, his spirit said, "Have fun, Robin! And remember, it's only money and you can't take it with you!" The spirit of Elvis Presley disappeared as he blended his energy into a large portrait. It was only then that I realized this machine was situated directly in front of a large portrait of Elvis Presley! Bob and I shared a good laugh about that, and it certainly wasn't lost on either of us that God had allowed "The King of Rock and Roll" to lead me to a machine that would pay generously by hitting "four kings". Yes, that was definitely one of those moments of intuition that left even me with a sense of awe and amazement. It is also a great example of God's own terrific sense of humor and irony. While that had been a working vacation for my husband and I, the Universe still gave us plenty of opportunities to lighten things up as we moved along our paths in life. And the money that was won, well, once again we knew that I would not have won that money if it weren't needed in our upcoming life's path. Clearly we still had more places to go and more things to do in Las Vegas, Nevada that would require us to have that money.

∞

The last day or so that we spent in the entertainment capital of the world was filled with more music as we attended a performance of the Platters, the Coasters, and the Drifters at the Sahara Hotel and Casino. Bob and I share a wide range of taste in our appreciation for music so that concert was another one that I was grateful to attend. These three groups had their roots in the early days of rock and roll back in the late 1950's.

There are so many talented singers and performers from that era that still draw a crowd more than fifty years later. Bob and I had grown up as young children in the 1950's but there was always some adult in our lives who was willing to share their own love and diversity in music with each of us. In my life and in my work as a psychic medium, I often find the use of music, as a healing tool for our spirits, minds, and bodies, is powerful if only we pay attention to the ways in which the Universe is guiding us to make use of that.

Healing comes to each of us when it is time in our own chosen life paths, but we also must stay open to all of the possibilities that the Universe offers. There was a very strong message coming through to me on that final full day that we spent in Las Vegas in July of 2005. My own moments of intuition were pushing me to go to Siegfried and Roy's Secret Garden and Dolphin Habitat. This was located on the grounds of The Mirage Las Vegas Hotel and Casino.

Mind you, I have personally gone to many zoos in various cities and states, as well as I have attended dolphin shows, including Sea World in Florida many years prior. I add this information because there was an overwhelming sense coming to me that the energy of Siegfried and Roy's Secret Garden and their Dolphin Habitat was something that I must experience before I left for home. The heat was still dauntingly dangerous but I knew that these places I was being guided to visit were for my own benefit and that could not be ignored. I had already worked hard to help many people with my psychic abilities while on this trip and yet I understood that these next attractions were for *me*.

Once again Bob and I rode the monorail system to allow us to get as close to The Mirage as possible. We needed to limit our time outdoors as we would be outside in the Secret Garden and the Dolphin Habitat for an extended period of time.

The first area that we were both interested in visiting that morning was the Dolphin Habitat. There were guides provided to each group that toured that area and so Bob and I joined about eight other strangers that day to learn more about these beautiful creatures. As we walked throughout the habitat, I found that the energy within that particular home to dolphins was quite positive, but with a strong sense of education and enlightenment. It was also evident to me that the healing I personally needed today was *not* going to be found in that area.

After a long, leisurely lunch break and some time spent gaming in the air-conditioned comfort of The Mirage casino, Bob and I both felt it was time to visit Siegfried and Roy's Secret Garden. For those of you who are not familiar with Siegfried and Roy, I will add here that they are world famous magicians who performed in Las Vegas for many years. They have been heralded as "Magicians of the Century" with a prestigious award of the same name. I would have to add that the energy of each of these two men is so positive and so intuitive that I am not surprised that God guided them through life so connected with animals.

The beautiful and highly intuitive animals that were a part of their long running magic act are important to these two men as seen in their commitment to preservation of the various species. Within the Secret Garden a patron was able to see exotic cats including white lions, snow-white tigers, and striped white tigers. One could also find panthers and leopards living amidst the tropical foliage of Siegfried and Roy's Secret Garden. There was also an Asian elephant named Gildah who called the Secret Garden home.

Bob and I entered the magical Secret Garden on a self-guided tour. By this I mean that each person was allowed to go through this jungle habitat in their own sense of timing as they observed the animals living there. As I stepped into the Secret Garden I was hit by a "wall of energy" so positive that I knew I had to find a bench to sit upon. Again, my own relationship to energy is strong and so I have learned to pay close attention to what I sense.

I sat quietly on the bench, adjusting to the amazing and healing energy that God allowed me to be in at that time. Eventually I stood and began to move slowly along the paths of the Secret Garden, as I was very focused on the animals within. Each animal has its own unique energy and spirit, just as humans do. And, just like a human being, there are animals that are quite positive, as well as those who sometimes feel quite negative to us. Each and every animal that I connected my energy with in the Secret Garden was so full of positive energy that it brought tears to my eyes. There was so much unconditional love energy flowing throughout that beautiful place that Siegfried and Roy have built as a habitat for their animals. Bob and I did not speak much within that place as we were both lost in our own sense of the experience. I feel blessed to have been brought there and said a silent prayer of "Thank you, God!" before I left that paradise.

We stayed out in the extreme heat for nearly an hour and I noticed that even the animals had the good sense to take it easy that day. When I felt as though my own healing process was completed at the Secret Garden Bob and I exited that place, bringing with us a profound appreciation for the lives and the work of Siegfried and Roy.

∞

With that I end this chapter of my book because it is clear to me that every part of that working vacation in Las Vegas, Nevada that was important for my readers to learn has now been shared. Oh sure, there were many more people that I passed on psychic messages to during our stay, and there were more places that we visited in the city of lights. But, the overall importance of that trip was to allow me to face my own fear in the extreme heat, while God guided me to keep moving forward on my own life path as I continued to help others. There had to be a complete and total trust in our own intuitive guidance throughout every step of that trip because only our Higher Power held the vacation itinerary in his hands. Bob and I had no clue what would happen as we chose to simply live in each moment as we kept our faith strong.

The money was something that, once again, God showed me will always be provided for in all of the needs in our life paths and occasionally a "want" will be fulfilled as well. You may wonder, "How much did money did they bring home with them from Las Vegas, Nevada?" Well, after following all of our guidance for those many days and nights; after all of the gaming wins and the gaming losses, after all of the wonderful meals, the concerts, and seeing the sights . . . we came home with $100 in Bob's wallet.

That working vacation in Las Vegas was never about us getting rich through any means of gaming. It was never about us having to sacrifice by spending our own hard earned money just to get to the city of lights so that I could do the psychic work that God was requesting of me. No, it was simply about bringing our own strong level of faith front and center as we trusted our Higher Power to give us all of the moments of intuition that we each needed for our own spiritual lessons and tests in the city that never sleeps.

CHAPTER SIX

Expiration Dates

Some days I find that the most profound thoughts come from the basic interactions of everyday life and my writing today stems from one such connection that began with my thirst for a glass of skim milk. I discovered that the thirst I had for a glass of milk soon led to a thirst for a deeper understanding of the importance of expirations dates in all things.

I am not a person who tends to drink milk often, preferring to indulge my liking for water and ice tea, but one day in early January 2012 the thought of a large glass of skim milk kept coming into my mind until I could no longer ignore it. My short walk to the kitchen to get that milk was easy and as I grabbed the gallon jug of skim milk from our refrigerator I was happy to see that there was a little less than half a gallon still left in the container. I anticipated my thirst would be quenched in less than a minute as I unscrewed the cap from the milk bottle. To my surprise I felt a sudden, but strong, nudge from my spirit's intuition to "smell the milk" before I poured myself a glass to drink. As a matter of habit I then turned the bottle around until I could view the "best if used by date" that is required by United States law to be stamped on all food, medicines, or perishable products. The expiration date on my gallon jug of milk was still five days away so my thinking mind reasoned that the milk should still be good but that nagging thought to "smell the milk" wouldn't leave my mind so I put the open bottle beneath my nose to breathe in the scent from the milk container. My reasonable expectation that the milk would still be fresh was soon replaced with the awful smell of sour milk. In spite of the fact that the expiration date should have insured a quality product for at least five more days, I had to face the fact that my thirst for milk would go unquenched until later. There was nothing I could do about it now as my situation that day did not allow for me to make a trip to the grocery store to buy fresh milk. A glass of ice tea would have to do, but I could not help but wonder "why" the Universe and my spirit had made a glass of cold skim milk seem so important right then. It would take several more moments of intuition and nearly three more weeks before I could comprehend all that my Higher Power was guiding me to understand.

In the days that followed I found myself intuitively guided to notice the "best if used by" dates on all of the food products in my refrigerator, in my cupboards and pantry, as well as on any of the new purchases that my husband Bob or myself made. As I reviewed all of the expiration dates I found that there were a few items that had overstayed their welcome in my refrigerator or my cupboards as the "best if used by" dates on them had passed us by. With no more thought than it takes to toss those now-expired items into the nearest wastebasket or recycle bin those things were dismissed of having any further value in my life. It felt good to let go of that which no longer served any positive purpose in my life and removing any product whose life span had come and gone felt right in every part of me.

The ability to sense the perfect timing for the life span of anything has long been one of the areas of spiritual growth that the Universe had been working hard to teach me about and even through the experience of sour milk I felt the strongest sense that something important was close at hand. I knew, deep within, that the idea that the milk in my refrigerator should have had a longer life span was simply an analogy for what lay ahead and the fact that I could not indulge my thirst for milk was not really what was important but rather that I "look within" to notice what God was really trying to reveal to me. I knew that there was something important, something vital to my life path that, I would soon have to accept would no longer be of any further use to me, no matter that I might otherwise have expected that "thing" to have a longer expiration date. I found myself pondering what that "thing" was and why my Higher Power was trying to get my attention through the basic analogy of food products that are good to consume one minute yet, seemingly overnight, we find that the consumption of that product could make us sick or even become the cause of our death as it had become negative in its composition.

∞

As the early days of January 2012 passed by I found that my thoughts were filled with examples of how the Universe incorporates the theme of expiration dates into nearly everything that any of us uses or experiences in our life paths. Everything and everyone has an expiration date that is predetermined by the Universe, by God, and we do not have the power to alter those dates in any significant way.

It became clear to my spirit and my conscious mind that God had brought me to a point within my own life path where I was feeling a most difficult task placed before me, one that I felt but that I could not yet put into words. I knew from previous spiritual challenges that I could certainly ask my Higher Power what "it" was but that I would only be given the information and the clarity of that which I truly needed to know, so I would have to be patient and allow the pieces of the expiration date puzzle to unfold. I did not have to wait long.

Information about the value of expiration dates came flooding into my thinking mind from my spirit and from our Higher Power, almost as if the value of that information was immeasurably important, but also necessary to maintain the sense of perfect timing in the Universe. I found that my spirit's intuition was being fully utilized by God as well as my psychic senses seemed to be bursting forth with all that I needed to access about the topic of "expiration dates." There was no doubt in my spirit or thinking mind that every single thing is linked to a sense of timing that will always result in a natural, spiritual conclusion. Everything—every person, every animal, every event, every relationship, every bit of microscopic cell matter, every emotion, every job, every spiritual lesson—will always exist in its Earthly form for exactly the length of time that the Universe allows for in order to maintain the perfect balance between spiritual growth and healing within the energy of spirit. To deny the existence or the importance of all things coming to an end is to deny any forward movement in one's life path. If all things did not come with their own inner sense of conclusion we would be left with a quagmire of "stuck spirits" all looking to our Higher Power for release. Nothing would move forward or progress spiritually if all things did not have a perfect sense of beginning and ending within God's universe.

Think of that cold glass of skim milk that I felt I really needed—nay, *wanted*—simply because the thought of it came so strongly to my conscious mind. As God surely knew, our milk had gone sour so there would be no quenching that thirst, instead the *real thirst* would be quenched; the thirst I have always had for spiritual understanding of the lives we are guided to live. Within my life path, the milk was simply a tool by which the Universe gained my attention in matters that would prove to be extremely valuable, perhaps in ways that only I can measure for myself as God guided my attention from the expiration dates of food and all things, to the expiration date of our beloved dog, Huck Finn.

∞

Huck Finn was a Jack Russell terrier that God brought to my attention in August 2010 when I was given a great deal of psychic information about three dogs that the Universe would be bringing into the lives of my husband Bob and me. At that time we had no dogs even though each of us had several other dogs brought into our lives, and the lives of our respective children, both before we met as well as after we had met and gotten married.

As two grown adults who were now grandparents Bob and I had even contemplated the thought that we might never have any more dogs as our children were grown and it would be nice to travel unencumbered by any dependent beings. Alas, that was not meant to be as God told me, showed me, and allowed me to feel the energy of the three very different dogs that Bob and I needed to accept into our life paths.

Huck Finn was to be the first of the three dogs that the Universe intended to bring into our lives, although God did not give me any specific sense of timing except that it would be quite soon. A month later, on September 13, 2010, through very specific and clear intuitive guidance, Huck Finn joined our family via adoption from a nearby animal shelter. He had been rescued from severe flood conditions in Iowa in July 2010 and through a series of shelter transfers, Huck Finn had been brought into a nearby city and to our attention. There was no doubt in my mind nor in my husband's mind that Huck Finn was the dog, the very spirit, whom God had revealed to me through psychic and intuitive guidance.

Since that time both Bob and I have paid close attention to our individual and collective sense of intuition about the three dogs that the Universe revealed to me in August 2010 and whom God did indeed guide into our lives and into our home, always in the sense of timing that only our Higher Power can determine as "perfect." There is much I could say about each of the three dogs, but it is Huck Finn that takes center stage at this time. I will focus on all that God has worked hard to teach me about him.

∞

Huck Finn was everything that God had revealed to me back in August 2010— and much more! He was energetic, yet a walk once or twice a day seemed to satisfy his physical needs; Huck wasn't like most Jack Russell dogs that I've heard about as he was not hyper in his activity level. That was a quite a positive trait to me as I loved a walking companion who was willing to accompany me no matter when I chose to walk. Bob, too, loved the idea of a canine walking companion and did his part to exercise the dog that God placed in our care.

The dog that God let me feel the energy of prior to his arrival in September 2010 was also a highly intelligent dog, a fact that delighted both of his owners, as he never seemed to tire of playing "hide-and-go-seek" with any of his toys or rawhide bones. Huck amazed us as he seemed to have the ability to scope out the most intricate hiding spots in every room and he could shimmy a toy into a spot where it "just fit" almost as if to camouflage it. "Hiding it in plain sight" was a thought that often came into my head whenever Huck Finn played his games; little did I know that phrase was also referencing the dark side that lurked within his spirit.

As with most rescue dogs that are adopted, Huck Finn came with a past that was sketchy in details. The veterinarians who had examined him during and after his rescue from the flooded areas of Iowa had determined he was approximately one and a half years old and that he was physically healthy.

The foster parents who took care of Huck Finn for our local shelter seemed to be very positive about him during our two visits to their home. Bob and I watched as both the foster mother and the foster father picked Huck up in his or her arms and snuggled together. Additionally we had brought our then six and one half year old grandson,

Devin, along for the visit, as we wanted to see if the dog we intended to adopt would be good with children. To our delight, Huck Finn and Devin hit it off immediately and throughout our two visits Huck showed no signs of aggression, not even towards two other smaller dogs that the foster parents had brought out into the back yard at the time of our visit.

My own sense of Huck Finn, at that time, was that he was a spirit who had the potential to bring so much positive energy and love into our lives but he also had exhibited a feeling of sadness, something I attributed to past issues for his spirit. Past issues in any being's spirit can come from past lives as well as the earlier years of his or her current lifetime. Animals are no different than people; we all come with our personal spiritual baggage, if you will.

During the adoption process Huck Finn came over to me and surrendered at my feet. This was remarkable to me, as I had been shown that in a psychic vision as a sign that would help us to further identify the dog we were meant to adopt.

Although Bob and I had already made our decision to adopt Huck Finn, the action of him surrendering to me felt like a solid validation that this was the dog we were meant to experience in our lives. In due time, all of the paperwork was completed and we paid for all of the required costs associated with Huck's adoption.

Happy to take our new family member home, Bob scooped Huck Finn up into his arms as I took charge of all of the paperwork. As we exited the gated and fenced backyard of the foster home, the foster mom stopped to mention to me that Huck did not always take to other dogs but that we could work to socialize him. She also mentioned that he would often have to be kenneled as he could get aggressive with some of the other foster dogs but she thought that he would do fine if we took time to bring him around other dogs and to give him opportunities to socialize in positive situations. Beyond that, any of his past experiences or potentially problematic behaviors were a mystery.

While Bob and I drove home with our newly adopted dog, we discussed what the foster mom had just revealed to me after the papers had been signed. We both had a slight sense of concern about her words yet all that we had observed about Huck Finn thus far had been quite positive so we made the choice to trust God's guidance that brought Huck into our lives and to let this experience be whatever it was meant to be.

Most of what we eventually came to know about Huck came from our personal connections with him and from all that our Higher Power revealed to us, little-by-little, as unbeknownst to us, Huck's time with us grew shorter. That's the trouble I sometimes have with the expiration dates on relationships between humans and all other beings that we love is that there never seems to be enough time to do all that we wish we could do before someone we love is called home to heaven to heal and to rest.

∞

My husband and I are fairly positive people who have a tendency to look at the bright side of life and I dare say that we can *always* see the light within any spirit—human or animal. One might say that is a wonderful gift to have but there are times—like now—when it can also feel like a curse. In the case of our dog, Huck Finn, I believe that both Bob and myself were willing to do all that the Universe asked of us as we truly wanted that dog to be a positive part of our lives. Unfortunately, we came to realize that Huck's placement in our life paths was meant to teach us more in the spiritual sense than to have a traditionally accepted "happy ending."

I think my friend Maggie said it best when I spoke to her in early January 2012 about the dark path that Huck seemed to have chosen that had been revealing itself over the past sixteen months that he had been in our home. As I explained to Maggie on the telephone one cold January day, "I can see the light in Huck's spirit and I can feel that he could be capable of so much good," she reminded me that, "Even though you can see the light in him, Robin, you can't make it shine for him. Huck has to choose to do that himself."

Maggie's comment hit me deep within and I knew that she was right. Neither Bob nor I could save Huck Finn from the darkness that he had been exploring since before we adopted him. Over time we had tried hard to encourage everything and anything positive that Huck did, always hoping that our unconditional love would conquer the dark place within him that so badly needed spiritual healing. A dark place in Huck's spirit that was not unlike the spirits of many of our human loved ones who can be kind and loving at times but then suddenly "go into the darkness" to a place where we are *not* guided by our Higher Power to follow.

The darkness I speak of can be a place of quick learning for most spirits, whether humans or animals, and can often lead to the understanding that it is best to walk our life path in the light, under the intuitive and loving guidance of our Higher Power, where we are kept safe and protected while also experiencing all of the spiritual lessons and tests we need. But I have learned through the course of many lifetimes that there are some spirits, both human and animal, who make a free will choice to step into the darkness. Some stay so long that it becomes harder and harder for them to feel comfortable in the light and so they behave in ways that allow them to disrespect—to push away—any and all spirits who stay in the light of God's path.

Whenever a person/spirit or an animal/spirit whom you love chooses to disrespect the guidance of the Universe and goes into the darkness, it is both frightening as well as disappointing. The disappointment can be nearly overwhelming as one realizes that the relationship they had previously "seen" was possible, within his or her spirit's mind, will never come to pass as that could only occur if all parties involved stay upon his or her spiritual paths, and always in the light of the Universe, of God. Any person or animal whose spirit chooses to be in the darkness can no longer be a part of any upcoming positive interactions; it is simply not possible. The Universe has already taught me that lesson well with regards to some of the human relationships that I have been guided to experience throughout my life.

In the canine sense, Huck Finn was the dog meant to teach me that concept and he did it well, as his spirit is a great communicator and his mind was sharp. Physically, Huck weighed in at sixteen pounds and was a healthy dog right to the end. His muscles were strong and lean, his teeth razor sharp. Huck's physical eyes and ears could detect the slightest movement, even in the dark, and the hearing in his physical ears was so keen that it appeared he made use of his own psychic abilities. There was no physical health issue with our Jack Russell dog that led to his recent death, just shy of his third birthday. No, the reason for the crossing of our beloved Huck Finn were choices made in the spirit and an exit path offered to him by God so that he could begin to heal.

∞

Over the sixteen months that Huck was our dog we observed behaviors and energy that could only be described as that of a bully. As a gifted psychic medium that can also communicate with animal spirits I was often guided by God to work with Huck's spirit in an effort to help him stay on his well-lit path. Too often Huck's spirit offered the excuse that he "was only trying to protect us" in those times when he was caught bullying others but that did not ring true to my inner self. I knew that the Universe does not require any of us to be kept safe through the actions and energies of those who choose negative behaviors of any sort.

I communicated all of that to Huck's spirit and mind as I urged him to let go of the negativity that was causing him to try to bully others, particularly other dogs and people with dogs. I found that, quite often, when we walked Huck Finn outdoors he would growl fiercely for a couple of blocks before we ever crossed paths with another dog and its owner. On one occasion Huck slipped his collar by somehow making his head and neck more compact, and without warning, he ran the distance of half of a city block, crossed the street, and attacked a dog that was just entering a park with its two human owners. Luckily, Bob and I were both out walking with Huck when this happened so Bob was able to run fast to pull Huck Finn off of the other dog. I ran, too, hoping that our dog would not cause injury to those people or their dog.

It took all of Bob's strength to gain control of Huck as I apologized to the other people involved. Neither Bob, myself, nor our dog, had ever crossed paths with those two people or their dog so there was no reason for Huck's attack. Everything happened so fast that it really shook me up because it allowed us to see what Huck Finn would do if he got loose. Clearly our dog was not choosing to be a dog that could be trusted to make positive choices and, if given the opportunity, was intent on attacking other dogs. Fortunately the other dog was able to hold its own against Huck and the dog's owners did not press charges.

I have always felt that was one of those times in life when the Universe tries to give us a glimpse of what lies ahead, even when we'd rather not "see" that in our lives or in the life paths of our loved ones, whether humans or animals.

Huck Finn's attack on a total stranger's dog led us to walk him with a standard, smooth choke chain type of collar as that did not allow him to slip out and, if he became aggressive, it would tighten. We had previously tried the soft harness method to gain control over him when he walked outdoors but that did not work. Huck seemed to put all of his energy into trying to escape from his collar and leash, often flailing around in an out-of-control manner that would require Bob or I to hold tight as we gave verbal commands to calm down or to sit but to no avail. There were times I would come home exhausted from my efforts to follow the intuitive guidance from God to walk my dog but I always focused on the positive strides that Huck Finn was making as most of us tend to do. Often we find that looking at the positives of the person or animal we love is done in such a way as to try to avoid facing the inevitable loss of that relationship in some way.

While my physical body kept working with Huck Finn's exercise needs, my spirit was keeping a close eye on any help that the Universe could provide us. All of this left my thinking mind confused at times because I could not make logical sense of Huck's choices, not in an Earthly sense and not in a spiritual sense.

Bob and I so wanted Huck Finn to "be" the good dog that we saw he was capable of being that I found myself stepping back into my spirit shoes to become the "observer" from time-to-time as I have learned that is helpful in dealing with any of the challenging spiritual lessons or tests of our lives. In my role as the spiritual observer, I was becoming increasingly aware of the fact that Huck Finn's energy was progressively more negative and that he was often choosing to disrespect commands that he had mastered early in our relationship. To that I added a keen sense of his willingness to ignore the needs of his physical body as his spirit wandered off into the darkness where he would refuse to eat or drink, often for two or three days, leaving his stomach to growl and complain loudly that it needed nourishment.

All of these choices, these habits if you will, were obvious and clear from the day we brought Huck Finn home to live with us yet God guided us to stay the course and to work hard to assist that young dog with his spiritual healing. It was only through the willingness of Bob's spirit and mine that we were able to stay the course with Huck Finn until the end of his chosen Earthly life experience.

∞

Two weeks before Huck Finn's death I was guided by my Higher Power to tune-in psychically as something important would be revealed to me. I have long ago learned to pay close attention to God when the sense comes through my intuition that I am to stop whatever I am doing and sit quietly as God speaks to me through my spirit's strong intuition, as well as he often utilizes the psychic gifts that he blessed me with. On that particular day I felt the need to immerse myself in the most positive energy within my home, which I believe exists in the room where I do my psychic readings for others, as well as I teach intuition and psychic classes in that space, too. Many times Bob and I had also been intuitively guided to take Huck Finn into that space as we tuned-in with God, angels, and spirit guides for any messages that the Universe felt we need at that time. That said, when God signaled me, I responded and brought Huck Finn along, as it always seemed to calm him to be in that amazing energy.

Relaxing meditation music filled the room as I took a few deep breaths to release any negative energy that might be held within my spirit, mind, or physical body at that time. Huck lay down on the floor near the source of the music and appeared to be relaxed, but he did not sleep. Instead, he seemed to be waiting patiently for me to "hear the news." The news that only God could show and tell me about in order that I might comprehend the seriousness of where our dog, Huck Finn, had now reached on his own Earthly path. The news that I would have to truly absorb in my conscious mind before I could speak of it to my husband, Bob, as it was life changing for our little family.

God did not waste words or energy as he described a fork in the road that was Huck Finn's path. To the left I was shown Huck's spirit's choices that were taking him more and more into the darkness where he would not respect Bob or myself, but more important was the fact that he *could not* possibly respect us as his owners because his spirit had chosen to disrespect God.

We all have the gift of free will choice along our paths but some spirits choose to go off of their chosen life paths and into the energy of darkness where God and angels cannot protect them. It is a part of the option of free will and one that can produce serious consequences to humans or animals. It is important to remember that a free will choice does not have to be negative or lead any of us into the darkness but can be a way for our spirits within to make use of all that we have previously learned to better our lives and the lives of others by making positive decisions that allow us to still stay on our well-lit paths. In any case, as God explained to me, Huck was at the point in his own life path where the Universe, whom I call God, required him to make a choice. If he chose to continue staying in the darkness and refusing to return to his life path then God would guide Bob and myself to take Huck Finn to our vet to be euthanized. It was clear and concise; there was no room for error in what I was given from God.

The right fork in Huck's path would lead to him be accepting of God's intuitive guidance for the remainder of his life, as well as there would be no more bullying or attacks on other dogs, but a part of that meant that Huck Finn could no longer "call the shots" as he had been working hard to do within our home. By that I mean Huck's spirit would have to accept the fact that his past behaviors, and perhaps more important, his current negative behaviors would no longer be accepted by Bob or myself to any degree. I "saw" psychically that Huck Finn had reached a point where he would have to be kenneled during the night and at times when we were not at home, both for his safety and for all others who lived in or visited our home. Huck was a dog, a spirit, whom God had given much freedom to, in spite of his many negative choices. As I saw, heard, and felt all that God was conveying to me in those moments I could not deny the fact that a strong sense of relief washed over me. For the past several weeks I had been telling Bob about a strong sense that kept recurring, deep within me, that made me feel as though it was no longer safe to allow Huck Finn to roam free while we slept. I saw psychic visions of him attacking us during our sleep and one of the visions showed Huck's jaw wide open as his sharp teeth sunk into my neck, going for the jugular vein, for "the kill" was the real sense I was given. In spite of my proven psychic abilities Bob had been unwilling to cage Huck at that point simply because he had not yet experienced enough of the negativity that Huck Finn seemed intent upon bringing to our individual attention.

Bob's hesitation to kennel Huck Finn at night was a reaction that I had observed in my husband through most of the days, weeks, and months that Huck lived with us as Bob is the kind of guy who does not really want to "be the bad guy" while I look at firm boundaries with people, animals, and spirits as healthy for all concerned. That said,

I have learned from past experience that I have to stay true to *my* intuitive guidance while allowing my husband and all others to stay true to theirs.

I found myself assuming a role of "watchdog" around Huck Finn, as I was the person who was home with him most days and evenings as my work is often accomplished at home. My gut instincts told me that Huck was sinking fast into the darkness and that he could no longer be trusted. My tune-in session with God in January 2012 only served to confirm what I had been sensing deep within my spirit—our lives with Huck Finn were rapidly changing and the outcome was *not* in our control. The Universe had given Huck's spirit a choice to make, not unlike the choices that appear in the life paths of humans from time-to-time. All we could do was wait for the signs that Huck Finn and God would provide to us; I could feel that it would not be much longer.

I should also note that the right fork in Huck's path also revealed that God's plan for him would be to live only another four years, as he would then be consumed by illness that would occur as a result of the negativity that he had chosen to absorb and to produce from all of those journeys into the darkness. It was evident to me that if Huck's spirit chose to stay with us—in the light of his path—we would still have to experience making the decision to end his life by having our veterinarian euthanize him to end his suffering in four years time. There was certainly no "win-win" solution here but I have learned to trust my Higher Power in all things, as no one could possibly know Huck Finn better nor understand all of the spiritual lessons and tests that were in his path.

∞

As I mentioned earlier, God had previously revealed to me that he would bring three dogs into our lives. Huck Finn was the first to come in September 2010. He would be joined, albeit briefly, by Ruby, a female West Highland White terrier in March 2011. Ruby's story is for another time but I can share with my readers at this time that she was a dog whom the Universe only intended to be with us for a mere three months and ten days before she was returned to the breeder, per the contract requirements.

God's guidance regarding the third dog continued until finally, a young pup we named "Jaden" joined us in mid-December 2011. Jaden was a mixed-breed dog, the product of a Lhasa apso dog crossed with a Cavalier King Charles Spaniel. My research about both of those breeds revealed that they are known for being good family dogs and are especially good with children and other pets.

Jaden was every bit as sweet natured and delicate in spirit as God had first revealed to me back in August 2010. Bob and I stayed true to God's guidance as we brought Jaden into our home on December 14, 2011, and we prayed that Huck Finn would accept her into our home the way he had accepted Ruby's arrival and departure. We hoped that our "good Huck" would be the one to stay with us and that he could become a positive role model for young Jaden.

Sadly, our hopes were dashed almost immediately as all of the aggression and negativity that Huck Finn had revealed towards all of the dogs outside of our home was now brought *into* our home. The Universe had brought Jaden to us at that time so that *we* could feel what it was like for others whose dogs crossed paths with Huck Finn. I can only say that it was ugly, ugly energy and behavior that he inflicted upon her and upon us. Snarling and growling in the darkest, most menacing way imaginable, almost as if he was possessed, became Huck's new normal. Teeth bared with eyes so full of hate, so full of darkness, that they left no more room for doubt in Bob's mind regarding Huck Finn's intentions.

My husband and I had now been brought to the same place of understanding with regards to our Jack Russell terrier, Huck Finn. We knew . . . *we knew* . . . that no amount of positive reinforcement or exercise was going to make any difference; our Huck Finn was gone and in his place was the spirit of Huck now gone to the dark side.

Awful . . . ugly . . . senseless . . . were some of the words that came to mind as God seemed to be speaking to me—loudly, and several times each day—in an effort to help me keep Jaden, Bob, and myself as safe as possible during those last five weeks of Huck's life. Our nerves were on "high alert" as we had to keep a close watch on Huck Finn for signs of aggression while also trying to incorporate a young puppy, just four months old when we got her, into our home and our lives. To say all of this was difficult would be an understatement but somehow, each of us persevered in the most positive ways that we could.

Jaden's spirit is one to be commended, as Huck's treatment of her was harsh, to say the least, yet she never gave negativity back to him at any time, no matter what she endured.

In the first five weeks Jaden lived with us she had to learn how to walk on various surfaces as she had lived her whole life in a cage with tiny squares of metal mesh on the bottom. She had to learn how to signal to go potty and had to learn where it was appropriate for her to go as she had been used to going in her cage.

Jaden had not been outside before and it was like watching a small, innocent child romp through the snow when she first got to experience it. This is a dog whose spirit embodies unconditional love and it is at once amazing, as well as humbling. Without a doubt Jaden has the lightest spirit's energy that I can ever remember feeling and it leaves both Bob and myself so grateful to have her in our lives. Perhaps in another lifetime Huck Finn would have felt the same but his path this time did not allow for him to enjoy a spirit whose energy was in such contrast to where he had now taken himself. As dark as Huck's spirit, mind, and body now were, Jaden's was the polar opposite—filled with God's light, unconditional love, and forgiveness. I could not help but wonder "why" the Universe had chosen that sense of timing to bring Jaden into our lives just as Huck Finn's spirit seemed to be spiraling out of control and deeper into the darkness. What good could possibly come from these two dogs' lives intersecting on the life paths of my husband and me? As I find is always the case, the answers always come when God determines it is time.

∞

Within the first three weeks that Jaden entered our home Huck Finn made the conscious choice to attack her in ways that allowed both Bob or myself the opportunities to bear witness to each of the six attacks—yes, I said *six* attacks—all sudden and unprovoked, and as vicious as Huck could manage before either Bob or myself placed ourselves between the two dogs so that Huck Finn could not cause any further harm to young Jaden. In all six cases it appeared that our beloved Jack Russell terrier had suddenly gone rogue and that we were left with no choice but to spring into action to save the life of our newest family member.

Twice the attacks happened when I was close by and observing the two dogs interactions; three times Bob was alone with Huck Finn and Jaden when he was forced to intervene. The sixth time occurred within six to eight feet of both my husband and myself leaving no doubt in our minds that Huck Finn was clearly *not* concerned about any repercussions that his aggression might cause for himself or anyone else in the family, as his behavior and his spirit's energy conveyed the sense that any disciplinary action on our parts was well worth the fear and anxiety that he was creating for the rest of us.

On one occasion I "saw" the analogy in my spirit's mind as God showed me how some humans and animals become so dark in their spirit's energy from negative choices that they begin to feed on the energy of chaos that they create. In essence, the negative behavior they choose to engage in creates the secondary energy of chaos and it is the chaos that they become addicted to and begin to crave.

In Huck's case, both Bob and myself were shocked and deeply disappointed as we have both had other dogs in our lives and had never known a dog who seemed to thrive on bullying others the way Huck Finn appeared to do. The very fact that we could see the light and the goodness in our Jack Russell terrier did not diminish the fact that he was choosing to viciously attack a young pup who in no way challenged him to be "top dog" among the canines in our household.

The physical attacks were just one way in which Huck Finn's spirit, mind, and body revealed his intentions as he also transmitted a wall of negative energy that could, literally, block Jaden's path as she tried to accompany Bob or I to the front door to go potty outside. I felt so bad for her as she was really trying hard to do the right thing and it was apparent that she was a smart dog who longed to please her owners. I found that there were many times in a day that either Bob or myself would have to correct Huck's behavior as he tried—repeatedly—to intimidate and block the paths of all of us.

More and more I found myself looking to God to help us understand Huck's needs, as well as "how" to provide firm, but loving boundaries for both dogs. I had taken a large black Labrador retriever to dog obedience classes many years prior and had been so successful that my canine partner and I had graduated at the top of the class. The training methods that I was taught had been applied many times, with many different breeds and sizes of dogs, providing me the proof that most dogs can become positive members of any household. Of course, I have been made aware through God's path for me in this lifetime that every interaction between humans or animals will always provide us with a spiritual learning experience no matter how long those beings are placed in direct proximity to our paths. In the case of Huck Finn, the sense of foreboding that his actions and energy created left me with the full understanding that something was going to happen that would make it obvious to Bob and I "which" fork in the road Huck's spirit had chosen. I could not shake the sense of intuition that I was going to be left somewhat hurt and extremely disappointed when all was said and done. And yet, I tried hard to start each day anew, always ready to give Huck Finn a fresh slate on which to write his tale, so to speak. I loved that furry, four-legged little guy and I try hard to forgive anyone's negative choices but the Universe has taught me that I cannot and should not ever forget the spiritual lessons that I have learned. One such lesson kept repeating itself in my thoughts, as Huck's time with us grew shorter; God's voice filled me with the words, *"Treat Huck Finn like the dog he is."*

I repeated God's strong words of intuitive guidance to Bob as well as my understanding of that recurring message: Huck Finn's spirit, mind, and body were not making positive choices that were bringing any sense of good or positive feelings to Bob, Jaden, or myself, and as such, he could no longer be given the sense of freedom and open-ended trust that he had long received within our home. In short, this was not a dog that deserved special perks and it was clear to me that he needed to be confined in a kennel or dog crate for the safety of all of us. I knew the time had come to enact that strong sense of intuition that I had expressed to my husband a couple months prior, even before Jaden had arrived, and this time Bob was in full agreement; Huck would be kenneled when we slept at night, kenneled when we left the home, and we would keep a unified sense of healthy but loving boundaries for all concerned. If there was any chance that Huck Finn's spirit would choose the well-lit path that God had provided for him we knew we had to do our part. We would do all that we could to "save" our dog but it was also time to give him up to God, as it was truly not in our hands any longer. By that I mean that we had to trust God and not allow any of the negative choices that Huck (or any other spirit) might make to deter us from what we were feeling was good and right in our lives.

Even as all of these dramatic events were unfolding, Bob still had to go to work at his job in a local school district during the weekdays, and I had already begun writing this, my second book. Additionally I was aware of several psychic readings that were scheduled for me to do for clients as well as all of the normal chores of daily life. To that I added the strongest sense of determination that I was not going to leave Jaden stranded in her path; she would be given all of the same positive opportunities to learn and to grow that Huck Finn had been given when he joined our family. Both Bob and I were committed to being a positive force that was not willing to buckle under for any more bullying from any source, be it human or animal. If Huck Finn was meant to stay with us we knew that both he and the Universe would make it abundantly clear to us. We also had the strongest sense of intuition that made it quite evident that the time for Huck's spirit's decision to be made would soon be upon us.

Each day that I was home with Huck Finn and Jaden I watched, listened, and felt the energy in each of them as well as I took note of the exchanges of energy between their two spirits. To that I added all of the personal interactions that I had with both of our dogs as well as I was guided by God to factor in Bob's experiences within the family unit. If God were keeping score I can only imagine how poorly Huck scored on the positive scale at that time of his life but he surely would have won the prize for top score in negative choices and accomplishments! Meanwhile, poor

Jaden seemed to be working hard to forge a positive place within our family even as she appeared to tread lightly around her older canine brother, Huck, who was obviously choosing a path of darkness.

∞

On Wednesday, January 18, 2012, I took both of our dogs outside to potty in the late afternoon. To that point in the day I had noticed that Huck Finn was still baring his teeth at Jaden and at me while growling in quiet undertones, almost as though he knew his behavior was unacceptable but he had to have the last word. At each infraction Huck knew that he would have to spend some time locked up in a dog crate that we only used for times when our intuition led us to believe that Huck needed a "time out" for the safety and well-being of all. It should be noted that the crate we were using was not his sleeping crate and was large, roomy, and well ventilated. That said, I would have to say that it had been one of Huck's better days in several weeks, yet I was taken completely by surprise at what happened next.

After completing his or her specific potty needs, it was time for Huck Finn and Jaden to join me in the warmth of our home. While outdoors each dog had their own tie-down cable that allowed them to roam our front yard within a reasonable distance while keeping them approximately six feet or more from the street and the neighbors' yards. Most of the time we put Jaden out to potty first as she was a puppy and did not yet have the sense of control over her bladder or bowels that Huck did.

For the most part Huck seemed to understand that routine and usually cooperated by waiting patiently for his turn.

Occasionally Bob or I felt that we should put both dogs out to potty at once as a way of acclimating them to one another. The behaviors we observed in those times was what I would describe as normal canine behavior and no attacks every occurred during those outdoor potty times. Potty time at 4:30 in the afternoon on January 18th was no different but the behavior between the two dogs immediately thereafter *was* as I washed my hands in the bathroom and returned to the living room. It was then that I saw the two dogs play and interact in the most wonderful, positive manner that it nearly took my breath away. I had to sit down in my wooden rocker and just "be still" as my spirit's voice whispered to me, not wanting to disrupt the delightful romp and playful interaction that was taking place in my nearby dining room.

Around and around the dining room table the two dogs ran, stopping occasionally to bat their paws at one another and gently nip in the way that dogs do when they are enjoying the playtime. I had witnessed Jaden play by herself many times as well as she had tried to engage Huck Finn on a few occasions when he was in a better mood but, until that moment, he had always turned away and remained staunchly removed from any interaction save for his choices to bully. I felt such a sense of joy in my spirit's heart; could this be a sign? Was Huck Finn finally choosing to return to his spirit's path? Would he finally leave the darkness that had become his near-constant companion?

As those thoughts whirled around in my mind, the two dogs finally came to rest, tired from the exuberant level of play that they had just engaged in. My gaze did not leave our dogs as they lay down within a few inches of one another, panting and tired from their playful romp. What happened next took me to another level of surprise and delight as Huck Finn turned onto his back and assumed a full surrender position that was clearly aimed at Jaden. I was not expecting *him* to surrender to *her,* as she had given no indication thus far that she wanted to be the dominant dog within the home. And if that wasn't confusing enough, I sat in my rocking chair and had to bear witness to Huck Finn surrendering not just once . . . not twice . . . but a total of eight separate times in a row.

By late evening, Bob and I would take note of three more times that Huck assumed the canine position of surrender to Jaden. His actions defied any sense of what we had come to expect from him but adding to our confusion was the way he looked at her, as if he *finally* felt the energy of unconditional love that Jaden's spirit emits. The best way I can describe it is that Huck Finn behaved as though he was basking in "the Light," in God's light, and he couldn't seem to get enough of it as he tried to remain close to Jaden. There were no more attacks that night and no more negative behaviors. I slept fairly well that night, as I had been unable to do for several weeks prior.

The next day was fairly uneventful until I brought Huck and Jaden indoors again after their late afternoon potty break. Once again I had gone to the bathroom to wash my hands, stopping in the kitchen afterwards as I realized I needed to take a decongestant pill for my allergies.

Standing at the kitchen cupboard I became engrossed in my own thoughts as I tend to when I am working on a writing project. Often times an idea for a new chapter comes to mind and I have learned to pay close attention to the voice of my spirit's intuition. Deep in thought, I was suddenly and abruptly brought back into the moment as the sounds of our two dogs fighting came to mind.

At first I was startled as I could not comprehend what I was hearing: a ferocious and deliberate attack by Huck Finn on Jaden as she squealed and yipped, trying to get away. It was almost as if my conscious mind could not register the sounds I was actually hearing because, only moments before, I had left the two dogs as they were starting to play and romp in the dining room. In fact, I had actually smiled to myself as I had observed Huck Finn was the dog that had begun to play that time and Jaden seemed only too happy to join in the fun.

What had started out as playtime had suddenly turned into a chance for Huck to mount a serious attack on Jaden as neither Bob nor I was in the immediate vicinity to defend the young pup and Jaden's small jaw with tiny puppy teeth was no match for the strong jaws and full-sized teeth of an adult Jack Russell terrier such as Huck Finn.

With the awful sounds of canine violence ringing in my ears I hurried through the kitchen and made my way across the dining room to where the two dogs were in a heated, one-sided battle. The sounds that Huck had been emitting were the kind of dog noises that one instinctively recognizes as so full of aggression as to cause injury, even death, to another being. I knew that I had to save Jaden from any further harm, no matter if Huck turned his violent rage on me or not.

As I reached the two dogs Huck suddenly paused and it gave me just the opportunity I needed to grab him under the collar, directly behind his head, so that if he tried to bite I could lift him up on his hind legs. As I did that I also let out a loud and firm, "NO, Huck! NO!"

In the days before that horrible attack I had been intuitively guided by the Universe to look up information on the Internet about how to handle aggressive dogs, specifically to read and note the gesture that I have just described. I detest violence in any form as I, too, have been on the receiving end of the physical anger from a few bullies in my lifetime and in that way I felt a kinship to Jaden. Just as I did not deserve to be attacked and beaten by human bullies, she did not deserve to be attacked and beaten up by a canine bully. Fortunately my response to Huck Finn's aggression took him by surprise and he immediately let loose his grip on Jaden as she quickly ran away, cowering near my favorite chair in the living room.

I held tight to Huck's collar and bent down slightly as I led him to a roomy dog crate that, unbeknownst to me at that time, would become his residence for the remainder of his life. Huck Finn did not hesitate when I opened the door and said, "Kennel!" as the look in his eyes told me he was fully aware of his choices and the consequences that came with them. The latch on the crate was secure but I found myself bending down to give it a tug just to make sure Huck could not escape the confines to which he was relegated before I left the sunny, spare room that housed all of the dog kennels and supplies.

Returning to the dining room area I found Jaden, visibly shaken, with a look in her eyes that said, "*Why? What did I do to him to deserve all of that?*" I took a few steps towards her so that I could comfort her when suddenly she began to vomit in such a way that the liquid contents of her stomach projected over a large area. All of the drama and upset had occurred shortly before the dogs' dinnertime so the little ten pound dog had nothing left in her. I scooped her up and placed her in a secure, portable fencing area for puppies that had been set up in a far corner of our kitchen and went to work cleaning up the mess in the dining room.

As I cleaned up my dining room carpet I could not help but notice that Huck had been completely silent since the attack while Jaden was now whining and whimpering, no doubt wondering why she was now penned up and what she had done to deserve this treatment. During the cleaning process I asked God to help me gain clarity about Huck's choices as I could feel my last good nerve was on edge. I have lived in stressful situations during my life with people of various ages who I have felt made some pretty negative choices and God knows well that he has brought me to a place of spiritual understanding where I know I do not ever have to accept that negativity again. No human, no animal, *no one* has the right to inflict negative free will choices on anyone else. The consequences of that kind of energy and any negative choice of action, will always be owned by the originator, and in this case, by Huck Finn.

God did speak clearly to me as he again showed me the two forks in Huck's life path but this time I was given the sense that it was time for Huck's decision to be made and reminded that the decision was between his spirit and God. All we could do was keep our faith strong and be vigilant in staying open to God's communications. And as I relayed the events of the day to Bob later that night I heard myself saying that it was time to call the vet to find out what would be involved if Huck would choose to exit his life path now. Bob nodded his head in solemn agreement as he, too, felt the weight of Huck's journey into darkness descending upon us all.

∞

Friday morning, January 20, 2012, began as most days do for me—taking our dogs out of their respective kennels and outside to potty so we can begin the day anew. Huck Finn had been offered food and water in the confines of the larger dog crate the evening before but he had only eaten a couple of bites before he was taken out to potty and then transferred into his regular sleeping kennel.

Hope has a way of creeping into my heart and mind, even at times when things look bleak, so I was willing to keep working with Huck as long as God guided me to for I felt no one knew that dog as well as our Higher Power, Bob, and me. No professional dog trainer could possibly know Huck Finn's path in life the way God did because our beloved dog's spirit had been placed into this life by our Higher Power for spiritual growth that involved not only Huck's spirit, but the spirits of all who came into contact with his chosen energy, whether that was positive at times or to the extreme in negativity.

I was steadfast in my own faith and had seen too much proof of spirit to allow doubts to creep in to my mind. No matter which fork in the road Huck's spirit chose I knew that no action would be taken without God's direct and clear communication to both my spirit and to Bob's as it is only through the perfect timing in the Universe that any of us come into our respective lives as well as we leave our Earthly lives.

Within fifteen minutes of Huck Finn and Jaden being let out of their separate sleeping kennels the true sign of Huck's choice in his path was made clear—Bob and I would have to take him to our vet to be euthanized.

Huck had gone out to potty and returned quickly, followed immediately by Jaden. It had sleeted and then snowed the evening before so our front steps and sidewalks were slick for me to navigate though the dogs did fine. As each dog returned to the large, enclosed front porch of our home I unclipped their individual tie-down lines from their collars—Huck first, followed immediately by Jaden—and then both dogs sat on the porch floor waiting for me to open the front door that led into our living room. My sense was that the dogs should *not* enter the interior portion of our home without me due to the seriousness of Huck's attack on Jaden the day before, but before I could take them inside I had to untangle the tie-downs at the bottom of the front steps.

I looked at both dogs and they appeared to be calm at that moment; I then spoke aloud to Huck Finn, reminding him to behave himself while I stepped outside. He looked at me and I could sense he got the message but something told me to back out of the front door so that I could keep an eye on the dogs.

Due to the size of our exterior, concrete, front porch stairs, I could only take one or two steps before I reached the first step on the stairs where I had to turn around so that I could grab hold of the handrail to avoid slipping on the icy steps. In the split second as I turned my gaze away from our two dogs, Huck Finn made the choice to attack Jaden for what would be the eighth . . . and *last* . . . time.

The tie-down cables left my hands as I hurried back into the front porch as quickly as the icy steps allowed, disgusted at the energy that I felt coming from Huck Finn and sick with worry about Jaden. Once again I had to step into the ugliness of what Huck's spirit, mind, and body were choosing to bring into our lives and to hold tight to his collar as I quickly grabbed his leash that was hanging on a hook nearby.

I secured him as tightly as I could to an immoveable metal object that was screwed to the wall of the porch by wrapping his leash around it and tying it down. In that very moment, the choice that Huck Finn's spirit had made was revealed to me by God, with no room for indecision on my part or on Bob's part when he learned of Huck's actions. As I looked into the eyes of the Jack Russell rough coat terrier that I had come to know and love I knew that it was time for Huck Finn to go home, to be with God so that he could truly heal. The truth of Huck Finn's choice hit me so hard that it felt as though my spirit's heart would break.

∞

The rest of the day was spent making arrangements with our veterinarian who would assist God in bringing Huck's Earthly life to a peaceful end. Bob and I talked several times by phone that day as he was still obligated to stay at work until 4 o'clock but the sadness we each felt was front and center.

I spoke to my daughter-in-law, Amanda, who graciously listened to me as I tried to update her on the events that had unfolded to bring Huck Finn and us to such a place within our lives. Sobs wracked my body as the emotions I felt came from deep within my spirit. It seemed as though the tears would not end, but eventually they did, allowing me to further discuss Huck's impending death with my oldest son, Brent, who had a real soft spot for both of our dogs.

Brent's intuition gave him the same sense as he, too, had witnessed Huck's decline over the sixteen months that we had him in our lives. Brent is a real dog lover, too, and yet, Huck's behavior towards other dogs had always seemed in stark contrast to the loving Huck Finn that was kind and gentle to all of the grandkids.

No one who had come to know Huck Finn within our home could comprehend the way that dog could suddenly switch back and forth between the energies of positive and negative . . . good and evil. And that is the level of darkness that Huck's spirit had brought himself to: a place where evil actions are perpetrated against others, especially those humans and animals whose spirits within are quite positive. I have come to recognize that energy as the Universe had previously guided me to work on several missing persons cases in which those who had perpetrated heinous crimes against others, particularly children, were doing so from a chosen place of darkness, a place where his or her spirit had made a free will choice to go.

My spirit did not have to convince my conscious mind that Huck Finn's crossing to be with God at this time was best for all as my life path had already taught me to trust God implicitly. Both Bob and I were given the full sense from our personal conversations with God that we could not push away the responsibility that we had been given as Huck's owners. We could not simply "dump" Huck and his serious spiritual behavioral issues on some other family.

We could not bring him to a shelter or to the Humane Society because God made it clear to us through all of the spirit connections involving Huck Finn that these behaviors had been progressively getting worse since Huck was brought into this current lifetime as a young pup and that nothing and no one could stop his choices. If we chose free will and ignored God's clear guidance to euthanize Huck at that time, then another animal or perhaps a human baby would be attacked, possibly killed, by Huck's actions. There was no wiggle room in the intuitive guidance from our Higher Power; the expiration date on Huck Finn's life had come due and we needed to respect his spirit's right to exit his Earthly life.

∞

Huck Finn's Earthly life came to an end in the late afternoon hours of January 20, 2012, and as we drove away from the veterinarian's office in our car, God comforted me with the news that Huck had arrived safely; his spirit had crossed over and was now choosing to be with God.

I was told that Huck Finn's spirit was happy—greatly relieved was the strongest sense I felt—and that he would be kept in his own energy so that all of that negative energy that he had taken in from the darkness would not be dumped into any other spirit. The Universe assured me that Huck Finn's spirit had now chosen to heal.

Relief and sadness washed over me, followed by another round of tears, but I knew that Huck's life and his time with us would not be wasted for there was much to take away from our shared experiences.

Over the next few days Bob and I had many discussions about Huck Finn as well as my deepest thoughts and feelings emerged about the spiritual lessons and tests that we had just completed with Huck's crossing over to heaven.

One thought repeated itself and that was about a brief spirit connection I experienced on that Friday afternoon, just a few hours before Huck's death. My son Brady's spirit spoke to me as "thoughts within my spirit's mind." Brady's spirit had been firm, but unconditionally loving, as he said, "Don't hate Huck, Mom. Try to think of him like me, like how my spirit felt when I chose to die. If Huck could, he would end his own life but as a dog, he can't do that, as his path doesn't allow for him to run in front of a car or to fight with a bigger dog that could kill him. You have to trust God and respect the choice that Huck Finn's spirit has made; let him come home, Mom."

All that my son's spirit conveyed to me during that short spirit visit rang true and I assured him that I did not hate Huck but rather I felt such an overwhelming sense of disappointment and sadness. Immediately I related it to what I have experienced with so many people and one other dog as I "saw, heard, and felt" the same kinds of energy in them that I had come to know in Huck Finn.

The images of those people and the one other dog, Ruby, came flashing through my mind as God reminded me of how many times he had already proven to me that no matter how much light I can sense in another being, I have no power that can make those humans or animals choose to walk in the light or to "be the Light." God reminded me that any being that makes a free will choice to leave his or her path of light goes into a place of darkness that will teach them much, but during the time any spirit disrespects the path that the Universe has placed them upon, they are also disrespecting God. And if a spirit chooses to disrespect their Higher Power, then there is no other spirit—human or animal—who will be shown respect to any degree unless and until the offending spirit makes the choice to return to the light, to God.

There is a very positive end to Huck's story in that my son Brady's spirit made another connection with me, just three days after Huck Finn crossed over. God allowed me to "see, hear, and to feel" that Huck Finn's spirit was now with Brady and that God was allowing my son's spirit to assist in Huck's healing process on the other side. As I heard and felt the news, a sense of relief and of unconditional love washed over me as I "saw" Huck's spirit running alongside Brady's spirit and there was no mistaking the smiles on both of their faces. My son and our dog are together with God; they are happy, and I can once again feel the goodness returning to life.

And Jaden—well, she's a little bundle of love and I cannot see or feel an end to that. To her credit she has maintained her positive outlook on life and loves to socialize with other animals and their owners. Adults and children alike seem to be drawn to her kind and playful ways. I look forward to the spiritual lessons and tests that Bob and I will share with Jaden as we continue to move forward on our life paths but we will always keep Huck Finn in our hearts.

CHAPTER SEVEN

Out of the Mouths of Babes

Within my life path I have been blessed to have so many opportunities of proof of spirit that it has left me with absolutely no doubts that a Higher Power exists and that we are all connected in spirit. Many people have told me that they would love to be me as I have such a unique life, but I know those words are simply being expressed in moments when that particular person has been opened up through his or her own proof of spirit experiences.

For some people there may only appear to be one or two occasions during which the forces of spirit, and the Earthly proof that reveals such activity, come together in such a way that spirit comes to life. It is in those fleeting moments that the Universe, whom I call God, has "opened up" another person so that he or she must find a way to make sense of what they have just seen, heard, felt, smelled, or tasted as no traditional Earthly explanation will do. In this way, the energy of faith comes alive and begins to grow ever stronger as it turns to the Light for nourishment and for ways by which it can be challenged on the Earthly plane of existence, yet can never be extinguished.

When I think of the word "faith" my conscious mind goes straight to my spirit's heart because that is the place where my faith in a Higher Power began to seed and take root. I know that this happened in a previous lifetime as I have always had a strong sense of faith in my current life path, even as a small child. Now mind you, I did not walk around talking about the ambiguous energy of faith, nor could I define what it meant to me it until recent years. No person could have looked at me and said, "Oh, now there's a child . . . a teenager . . . a young woman . . . a grandmother . . . who has strong faith!" Faith is not so much about a person's Earthly appearance, or the life path that God has placed them upon but is an energy that resides within us as individual spirits of the Universe. As I have come to know, faith is the healing balm of the Universe, of God, and the ways by which it can flourish within each of us are many and varied. That said one of the ways that has always deeply affected me and allowed my faith to grow ever stronger is when proof of spirit has been revealed to me through the youngest and most innocent among us. It is the proof of spirit that comes out of the mouths of babes that always gets my undivided attention, as I believe it is proof of a higher power in its purest and most loving form.

It would take a hardened heart to turn away from the unconditional love, the absolute trust, and the unbridled faith that comes when proof of spirit is made visible through the spirit, mind, and body of a baby. I am a fortunate being to have been privy to many such spirit connections but I will share only three of those with my readers at this time, as these are just a few of the many spirit connections with babies that have resonated so deep within my own heart thus far.

∞

The first of these spirit connections involving babies occurred approximately three and one half months after the death of my son, Brady. As one would expect, my grief was acute at that time of my life as was the grief of all of Brady's loved ones. Every day seemed more difficult that the last, yet the demands of life and family did not allow for most of us to wallow in our grief, nor did the Universe guide us to give up on life. I know from my personal perspective that it felt as though God had not only taken my son too soon, but that as Brady died a whole lot of other life changing events were occurring, and at breakneck speed. Decisions had to be made that would not only affect my life path and the life of my husband, Bob Dedeker, but also the life paths of my other two sons, Brent and Blake. I was grateful for my strong intuition, especially during the days, weeks, and months that followed Brady's death, as it was the inner compass that I truly knew I could depend upon as it had proved itself to me throughout my life. No matter how chaotic and out of control life felt once I discovered my son had chosen to die, my intuition was the ballast that kept me afloat.

At the time of Brady's death my oldest son, Brent, and his wife, Amanda, were looking for a place to live as their prior rental situation had not been a positive one and had forced them to move to where their two young children, Autumn and Gillian, could be kept safe. Autumn was two months shy of her fifth birthday when her beloved uncle Brady died, and Gillian was a mere babe, just ten months old, who had not had much opportunity to know this uncle of hers named "Brady." In fact, Gillian had not seen Brady since she was two months old as he had been working hard to beat his addictions to substance, particularly to cocaine.

Brady knew that his older brother Brent did not want any person who was under the influence of substance to come anywhere near his two children. Brent was trying hard to keep strong boundaries in place for the safety of his young family. And as much as Brady loved being an uncle to Autumn in her earlier years, by July 2000 he had made the conscious choice to face his personal demons of addiction head-on and had been working hard to do just that for several months when he, apparently, reached his own "brick wall" on his life path and could not "see" a future for himself beyond where he was at that time.

I use those terms to describe how my son's spirit, mind, and body "saw" his life path in late December 2000 because that is the way his spirit has explained it to me from the other side, from heaven. Brady felt it was his time to die, to cross over, because he could no longer "see" anything left in his life path. In as much as his death was the most painful thing I have ever experienced, I do understand his spirit's description because it is one that I have come to recognize through the course of my work as a psychic medium.

There have been occasions when God has guided me to work with the family members of a person who has ended his or her own life and the sense of energy is always the same when God brings the spirit of the person who chose to die through to connect with me. There is always the sense that, for whatever reasons were compelling that person to end his or her life path, the common denominator is that the person's spirit and mind could not "see" a life path that continued on any further. In Brady's case, it did not matter whether or not any of his loved ones wanted him to be a part of our futures, of our lives, as the Universe has made it abundantly clear to me that Brady lived and died the life path he was meant to experience and all healing had to begin with acceptance of that spiritual fact.

To accept the death of a loved one from any cause often requires the proof of spirit connections that only our Higher Power can provide, and in the right sense of timing to allow us to absorb the meanings behind those connections. In spite of my strong psychic abilities I, too, am a person who required that same proof of spirit in order to move forward through the process of healing from deep grief brought on by the death of my son.

∞

As I have previously mentioned in my book, we can all experience spirit connections through the dream process and these can often be so detailed that it leaves a person shaking their head in disbelief. In mid-December 2000 I had one such vivid dream message that was brought to me through spirit connections while I slept, a message that left me no doubt that God has a plan for all of us, even when it may be a difficult one to grasp. I am talking about the kind of messages delivered to us via spirit connections that require a strong level of faith to help soothe and to heal us.

Approximately two weeks before I discovered that my son Brady had taken his own life I had a dream in which my spirit was listening to God. I "saw" God and heard him explain to me that my oldest son Brent, his wife Amanda, and their two small children would soon be living in the basement apartment of our home in Shakopee, Minnesota. My spirit felt confused and she reminded God that Brady was already living in the basement apartment of our home and it appeared to me that arrangement was working well for Brady as he was nineteen and one half years old—a young man by any standards—but a wise, old soul deep within.

Brady was also a talented musician so the basement apartment gave him a place of his own where he could practice his music at reasonable hours. In spite of his struggle with addiction, Brady was a fairly respectful person and had often remarked to me that he really liked my husband Bob and that he thought the three of us got along great. And aside from a few tumultuous years in his mid-teens, I would have to agree.

The dream continued on with God showing my spirit that Brady would be living "above us." What I actually saw was Brady floating in the upper level one-half story of our home that was situated above the main level of our home (where Bob and I resided). Our home in Shakopee was built in 1926 but the uppermost level had never been finished off to use as living space. Brady had been urging me for months to buy some building materials and he would do the work for us at no cost. Brady had worked for a couple of years in the construction industry so he had picked up some knowledge about building and remodeling.

As God showed me the vision of Brady "floating" in the upper level of our home I suddenly saw his bright red Fender guitar in his hand. Of all of Brady's possessions, none were as important to him than his electric guitar. I took that as a sign that something was going to happen that would allow Brady to "move upstairs" because he wouldn't go anywhere without his guitar!

When I awoke the next morning I couldn't wait to tell my husband Bob about the detailed dream that I'd had. At that time I did not know that my son Brent and his wife were looking for a new place to live in, as they had not discussed it with me. I wanted to tell Brady about the dream but my gut instincts told me to "wait" as Brady could be impatient and I didn't want him to start on any finishing work in the upper half-story section of our home until I knew we had enough money to do all of the work. I finally had the chance to tell Bob about my dream later that same day, but also felt I needed to gain more clarity about the dream before I mentioned it to Brady. After all, I could not understand "why" Brent and his family would suddenly be moving into our home and I did not yet know how we could afford to finish off the uppermost space for Brady to live in. Good questions that I felt would be answered in time . . . but I had no idea that God's sense of perfect timing would reveal itself in a couple of weeks.

As interesting as I found that dream to be I could not yet know that the symbolism of God's message to me was that Brady would be "living above us" because he would no longer be living an Earthly life. I could not yet comprehend that my son's spirit would be making music from a heavenly place rather than from the comfort of our family's home. I could not yet know that my oldest son Brent would reveal to me that his young family had no place to go and was living apart at the time of his brother's death.

It wasn't until Brady died that I found out that Brent and his family had moved out of their prior living situation. It was when I spoke to Brent on the phone to give him the painful news of his brother's death that I learned Brent's car had broken down, forcing him to stay in the extended stay motel located next door to his employment. Amanda and the two little girls had found a temporary place to stay with a good friend of hers but the young family clearly needed a place that could provide a home for all of them.

My mind was reeling when I heard of Brent's plight that had coincided with his brother's death. I could not help but look back upon my dream, just two weeks prior, and wonder aloud, "Did God *know* Brady was going to die?" And if the Universe *did* know, how come God or angels couldn't have guided me through my intuition—in some way—that would have allowed me to save my son's life?" Tough questions to even think about but I would find that the answers would require a level of faith, of acceptance of God's plan for all of us that I did not realize I had within me.

∞

Brent, Amanda, and their two young children, Autumn, and baby Gillian, moved into the basement apartment of our home in the weeks soon after Brady's death. By mid-April 2001 we had all experienced so many major life changes in such a short period of time that it took every bit of inner strength that we could individually and collectively muster to keep moving forward in our lives.

One of the things that I had to personally attend to was to go through all of Brady's personal belongings and make the decisions regarding what to do with them. The amount of strength it takes to sort through another person's life possessions is, in my opinion, vastly underrated, because those items are not just "stuff" but they are the Earthly symbols of a life review for the person who died.

Brady was a legal adult by the time he died and most who knew him agreed that he was a pretty mature fellow for his age yet the amount of objects, of things, that he had acquired as an adult had been few. He loved his music so his collection of CD's went to his younger brother, Blake, who also shared Brady's passion for music. The red electric Fender guitar and a couple of amplifiers were probably my son's most prized possessions so my intuition told me to hold on to those for now. The guitar was actually the second red Fender guitar that Brady had owned in his short life, yet he had played it often. I would later be guided by God and by the spirit of my deceased son Brady, to "let go" of the guitar and amplifiers and to pass them on to Blake, as a gift meant for his healing, from God and Brady's spirit.

I cannot express in words how difficult it was for me to follow that bit of guidance from God and yet I recognized that the guitar that had brought Brady so much happiness would serve its best and highest purpose only if someone, like Blake, could play it. Adding to the difficulty of God's guidance to me was the fact that my son Blake was deep in his own spiritual lesson of substance addiction at the time the Universe and Brady's spirit asked me to pass the guitar and amplifiers on to Blake. Anyone who has ever dealt with the lessons of addiction within his or her life path, whether you are the addict or the enabler, knows that anything of real financial value often ends up in a pawnshop for drug money. Eventually my worst fears were realized as years later my son Blake's godfather called to tell me that Blake had admitted to pawning Brady's guitar. It was at that time when the Universe reminded me that Brady's spirit still has *his* red spirit guitar and is making beautiful music in heaven. God told me, gently but firmly, that I needed to let go—forever—of the Earthly symbol, the red Fender guitar, and so I did. To this date I have no idea what became of Brady's Earthly guitar but I am at peace because I know it's where God needs it to be.

As my task to sort through Brady's possessions came to an end, I was left feeling as though I had been "listening" to my son's spirit whispering in my ear so that each and every single item he owned would be given or donated to the person(s) or charity that he approved of. His older brother Brent loved to play video games with Brady since they were young children and the two of them still shared that bond at the time of Brady's death so all his video games and the machines on which to play them went to Brent. I make mention of these items only as a reference to help others understand that the spirits of our loved ones really do connect with us, even in subtle ways that can help us make difficult decisions after their deaths.

One of the most important Earthly treasures, in my opinion, are the photographs that each of us leaves behind for our loved ones to look upon in those times when our minds require more than just the images of our memories. In the case of my son's death, I was blessed with many photos that I had taken of all of my children throughout their entire lives. Some of those photos had already been sorted and labeled in photo albums; others were in frames that sat on my piano, or hung on the walls of our home. It is one of those framed grouping of photos that became the tool by which my granddaughter, Gillian, revealed to me her personal spirit connection with her uncle Brady.

∞

It was springtime, mid-April 2001, and though I had tried hard to keep myself sorting through my dead son's belongings I had come to an impasse regarding a frame that held several of his photos from when he was a baby through the age of approximately five years old. I have no idea why that collection of photos had caused me to get stuck in my grief but they did and so I could not bring myself to box up that particular frame full of photos nor could I come to a decision as to where I might hang them up in our home. Before Brady died the collage frame of childhood photos had hung on one wall in his bedroom but since his brother Brent's family had moved into the apartment space it did not feel right to me to keep those photos in that space any longer. I found myself stacking a couple of smaller boxes against one wall in our dining room and atop of those boxes I absentmindedly propped the framed photo collage of Brady as a baby and young child.

One evening soon after I found myself standing in the dining room as I spoke to my daughter-in-law, Amanda. She had come upstairs to ask me a question about something and had brought baby Gillian with her. As any grandmother would be, I loved to see my grandkids and tried hard to enjoy them even as the powerful grief caused by the death of my son Brady often lurked in the shadows of my heart and my mind.

Gillian had celebrated her first birthday six weeks prior but she was still not very interested in walking or talking a great deal. While her mother and I chatted, Gillian sat perched on Amanda's hip until the baby got bored and began wriggling in her mother's arms. Amanda set Gillian down on the floor and the baby began crawling furiously towards the small stack of boxes and the framed photos of Brady. Something deep inside me gave me the intuitive sense that I needed to watch and listen to my baby granddaughter, though I couldn't image why.

In a flash Gillian pulled herself up to a standing position, holding on to the top of the boxes as she looked intently at the many photos of her uncle Brady. Suddenly my thirteen month old granddaughter began pointing to each of the collage photos while she spoke, clearly saying, "Brady . . . Hi, Brady! Brady . . . Brady!"

I was stunned and moved closer to watch as she pointed her little finger to each photo and as she did, there was no mistaking that Gillian was able to pick out the exact person within each photo that was Brady, no matter how old he was in any of the photos. Keep in mind that she had not seen her uncle Brady for nearly a year by the time this took place and she had never seen him as a baby or a young boy. Additionally, those photos contained groupings of many other people, too, whom Gillian would also not know, yet she was clearly able to pick out Brady in each photo.

Amanda and I were both so amazed by what we were seeing and hearing that we forgot for a moment that Gillian had not yet learned to speak very many words yet, suddenly, she was repeating the name of her deceased uncle! That fact came quickly to my thinking mind and as it did I was also given the full understanding that Gillian had just shown us her own proof of spirit connection.

I told Amanda that I could feel Brady's spirit in the room with us, and that he was really happy because he had "talked" to his baby niece, Gillian, and she had repeated aloud all that he told and showed her with regards to those pictures. Amanda, Brady's spirit, and I were all so excited to witness all of this that I almost forget that Gillian had never yet said the word, "Grandma." Suddenly I heard myself chiding Brady's spirit saying, "Thanks, a lot, Brady! You should have taught her to say 'Grandma' first!" Of course, Brady's spirit laughed at me, just as he would have if he were still in his Earthly life and suddenly I knew that I had to hang that framed collage of young Brady photos in my dining room as a reminder to me that children are so open to spirit connections with the Universe, with angels, with spirit guides, and even with the spirits of our loved ones. Never a day goes by that I don't pass those photos and smile fondly at the messages brought through to Amanda and myself straight from an innocent baby and the spirit of her uncle.

∞

A couple more years would pass before the Universe allowed me to experience another powerfully moving spirit connection with a baby but this one was very different in its nature. My son Brent and his wife Amanda had become pregnant with their third child and the ultrasound tests showed that the child who would join their family was another daughter. For many months my son and his wife searched baby books and bandied various names about, never feeling as though they could settle on the right name for the baby that was coming to join them.

Through my work as a psychic medium I have come to understand that every spirit who comes into a life, whether human or animal, chooses the name that he or she wishes to be known by in that upcoming lifetime. Parents usually figure out what that name is through the simple process of intuition. In other words, the spirits of the parents connect with God and the baby's spirit to learn what name has been chosen. From there, most of us are able to get that information straight from our inner selves to our thinking minds, with occasional assistance from angels and spirit guides. However, in the case of the new granddaughter that was due to be born in late July or early August 2003, the chosen name was being kept a secret and my son Brent and his wife were stumped.

A couple of weeks before the baby's birth I awoke from a deep sleep, one in which I knew I had made a spirit connection with my baby granddaughter's spirit. I was made aware of the spirit connection through a vivid and detailed dream that had occurred just before I woke up for the day, which allowed me to have total recall of the dream messages.

Within the dream I "saw" the infant's face clearly and she described to me that she would "Look like you, Grandma!" when she was born. I will add here that, indeed, that baby girl was the spitting image of *my* baby picture when I was born, although we did not look alike beyond that moment.

I was also shown and told that the baby would have dark blond natural curly hair "Because I want curls, Grandma!" and that she was going to be very much a girly-girl who would enjoy dressing up, getting her hair done, and wearing a little make-up, too. I "saw" her little fingers as she showed me that she would love to paint her fingernails and even her toe nails, as she loved all sorts of colorful ways of expressing her female energy. Every single way in which my granddaughter's infant spirit revealed to me the truth of "who" she was has come to pass thus far. Of course, there are some things that were shared that I cannot yet write about as she has to bring those parts of herself and her life path out on her own, and in God's sense of perfect timing without any influence on my part, as only that would allow for the truest sense of proof, of validation.

The baby's spirit showed me an image of herself at about two years old, standing with her arm around her family's dog, Butt Kiss, a large boxer dog. The sense I immediately understood from the baby's spirit was that she and the dog would be "best friends"—and they were. She also told me and showed me that she would be a huge fan of the Star Wars movies which would be something she would share with both of her parents, but especially with her father, Brent. I can only say that this granddaughter of mine quickly became the youngest Star Wars fan I have ever met and she has seen every one of the movies multiple times, generally sitting by her father's side!

The last thing that the baby's spirit told me was that she wanted me to give her parents a message from her. I agreed and she told me that her name was to be either "Mara Jacqueline" or "Mara Jayne" or something that sounded a lot like that. She winked at me and smiled big as she said her parents would understand the message. With that, her infant spirit was gone and I suddenly awoke in my bed.

I was so excited to share the news with my son, Brent, and his wife, Amanda, that I jumped out of bed and got ready to start my day. Within a half an hour I was ready to visit with them so I went downstairs to the apartment and knocked on the door. To my surprise both Brent and Amanda were standing together, just inside the door, as if their spirits had guided them to be on hand for the news! I could not wait to tell them the good news about their daughter's spirit as I sensed the excitement of the baby's spirit nearby.

As soon as I finished explaining everything that the baby's spirit had revealed to me within the dream messages I asked my son and his wife if the names that the baby had given me rang true to them. They both loved the name "Mara" but didn't think that the middle name was Jacqueline or Jayne as neither of those felt right to them. Suddenly Brent's face lit up and he said, "Mara *Jade*! That's what her name is—it's Mara Jade!"

I was puzzled as to how he knew the middle name of "Jade" but he quickly explained to his wife, Amanda, and to me that the original Star Wars books have a character in them named Mara Jade, a woman who had not yet been featured in any of the movies. Brent's face was beaming and his wife was smiling, too, as the name for their new daughter had finally been revealed through the messages of her infant spirit to me, her Grandma Robin.

Mara Jade entered her Earthly life on August 5, 2003 and I was blessed to attend her birth but that is a tale for another time, another book. True to her spirit's word, Mara Jade is a beautiful girl with a head full of natural curly hair that won't quit, but most important is that she is a positive spirit who connects well with the Universe, with angels, with spirit guides, and the spirits of her loved ones. Mara Jade is yet another of my psychically gifted grandchildren, yet her path is unlike mine. I can tell you one thing for certain: just as Mara's spirit was capable of speaking out on her own behalf, even before her birth, so too will she assist other small children to speak out—loudly and clearly for themselves—as they navigate the life paths that the Universe places them upon!

∞

Lest you think that the only babes who speak to me in spirit or who make spirit connections are those within my biological family, I will share one last story of spirit connections that I was blessed to experience with the infant spirit of a very special baby boy.

It was through the relationship that I have with my daughter-in-law, Amanda, that the Universe guided me to meet a young woman that I will call "Mary Ann." Amanda and Mary Ann had lived next door to each other as children, each having brothers with which to share the joys and sorrows of childhood. With no sisters of their own, Amanda and Mary Ann soon recognized the energy of sisterhood resonating between their inner selves as well the start of what would become a life-long friendship. Now I am not referring to the kind of friendship whereby two people only share the best times of their respective lives; no, that would not define the deeper level of friendship that these two girls would ultimately share, as they became young women with families of their own. The friendship that the Universe has intuitively guided me to see, hear, and to feel between Amanda and Mary Ann is one that is very much like sisters who are best friends. They have laughed together, cried together, fought with one another over real or imagined slights, and they have had each other's best interest at heart in those times when a true friend is needed most. Mind you, I have certainly not been privy to all of the interactions between these two young women but, for some reason, God has brought them both into my life enough times, both separately and together, to allow me to know them well. And one thing that I have come to understand about these two younger women in my life is that they are bound together as spirit sisters, and as spirit friends, for the remainder of their Earthly lives.

To best understand the spirit connection between Mary Ann and Amanda requires a person to "step back in his or her own spirit shoes" in order to gain a broader perspective. These two women/spirits are ones who will always help to lift the other up when she is down, for any reason, while traversing the rocky roads of their respective life paths. Additionally, the Universe has revealed to me that these are two women whose spirits act as mirrors on occasion, to better reflect the energy and intentions back to one another. In this way they serve to act as the person, the spirit, who is willing to be truly honest with the other in times when other people might be unwilling to express the tough stuff, the kind of stuff that none of us really wants to express or explain to people whom we love. But it is only through the willingness of any person, any spirit, to be honest with another that allows us to truly grow in spirit.

As you, too, may have come to understand within your own life path, there are many times in life when each of us needs someone close to us, to "be the mirror" for our words, actions, intentions, and our energy. Each of us needs a least one person in our lives who is willing to not only stand beside us when times are tough but who must also be willing to stand in front of us as their spirit "mirrors" all that we have just put out in the Universe back at *us*. Some may call this "tough love," but I prefer to call it *real love* . . . unconditional love, and I feel blessed to not only have a few people in my life who have served as my spirit mirror from time-to-time but I have also been placed in the position where my Higher Power requires me to reciprocate as a mirroring spirit for many others.

To mirror the entirety of another person's spirit back to them is one of the most challenging spiritual lessons that I have personally participated in along my current life path but I would have to add that it has also been one of the most fulfilling because it has led to a depth within those particular relationships that cannot be reached any other way. In simple terms, we can only form deep and unconditionally loving relationships with others by being unconditionally loving as well as we must be completely open and honest. Not only must we be willing to accept others for the good, the bad, and the ugly that we all have within us, but we must be willing to be truthful as we reflect upon and return his or her energy to them in ways that the Universe requires of us, no matter what. In the case of Amanda and Mary Ann, I have seen, heard, and felt the willingness of both women to do just that as they have grown from young teenagers when I first met each of them, to adult women with husbands, children, and careers of their own.

Amanda is a few years older than Mary Ann and began having the first of her three children when she was only seventeen. A series of events had occurred in the lives of my son Brent and of his now-wife Amanda that led to the two of them making choices that brought a child and all of those adult responsibilities into the lives of two unprepared teenagers. The path for these two young parents had been defined by the Universe and, as we all must learn to do, they accepted the choices that they had each made, including the choice to become young parents.

As time went on it appeared as though Amanda and Brent were the kind of couple who need only to *choose* to have another child and the Universe would oblige. In other words, they did not experience fertility issues or difficulty in getting pregnant with any of the three daughters that they had together.

Throughout all of the births of Amanda's three daughters, her good friend and sister spirit, Mary Ann, was close at hand, always bringing cute little outfits for the girls, and remembering their birthdays. Auntie Mary Ann has been a real favorite and a special person in the lives of those three granddaughters of mine, one that I was glad to get to know on a personal level as well.

Mary Ann's life path was much different as her spirit and God had chosen a life path in which she got to work, travel, and to marry her husband before any children entered the rosy picture. At times my intuition and my psychic sense couldn't help but pick up on the fact that Amanda sometimes appear to envy Mary Ann's freedom and her lifestyle. In the same vein, there were times when a person couldn't help but notice Mary Ann sighing, with a wistful look upon her face, as she viewed the three beautiful, smart, and healthy children that God had already brought into the life of her good friend, Amanda.

As I have always noticed is the case, just about the time in life when any of us thinks someone else's life is so much easier or "better" the Universe reveals the truth. It is often in those moments of truth-filled intuition that we are left to feel ashamed of ourselves for feeling envious or jealous of another person or his or her life. It has been my experience that each of us will be faced with many challenges as that is the way we learn and grow in spirit.

∞

Mary Ann talked quite openly about the fact that she wanted to start a family with her husband; a child was at the top of her "wish list," and yet she did not experience the ease of starting a family that her life-long friend, Amanda, had. The strongest sense that always came to me to share with Mary Ann was that God would bring children into her life but that she had to trust in God's sense of timing and, that in Mary Ann's case, no artificial means would make that happen. Like most of us, Mary Ann's spirit was required to do a certain level of healing that only our Higher Power could measure, as well as the timing for any of us to bring a child into our lives is *always* determined by the Universe, by God.

No amount of wanting or pleading or begging will ever create life, as the life paths each of us must walk are so individualized, so perfectly timed, as to allow us to intersect paths with one another in God's sense of perfect timing. In Mary Ann's case, I believe that the Universe was intent upon bringing children to her but not before she experienced several false pregnancies, miscarriages, and failed in vitro fertilization attempts. In other words, the path to motherhood for that young woman was vastly different from that of her best friend whom God guided into motherhood as a teenager. One might ask, "Why? Why was the path of one woman becoming a mother so seemingly 'easy' while the other's path required so much effort, so much faith?" Of course, the answers to those questions are not all mine to know but one thing that comes immediately to my mind from my spirit is that *both* of the women have been challenged with difficult paths to and during motherhood.

Neither one of these two women has had an "easy" path yet their lives as mothers, or as women, could not be more different, thus adding to the challenge of being one another's mirroring spirit. It will only be through the many differences in Amanda's and Mary Ann's life paths that these two women will learn all the ways in which they are so much alike, as two spirits living the life of a woman, wife, and mother at this time in the history of the universe.

Both Amanda and Mary Ann will continue to be challenged by the spiritual lessons and tests that God places before them while at the same time they will each be guided intuitively to lend a helping hand to the other. They will continue to be tested to offer help and assistance while still allowing the other person to make her own choices, her own mistakes, and to be proud of her triumphs. These two women are in life paths in which not only they must work hard to stay connected, but so, too, must the children that God has brought into each of their lives as these children represent another generation of "sibling spirits" who will forge friendships and will mirror for one another.

All of this leads me to share the last of my spirit connections with a tiny baby spirit who was destined to become the first of Mary Ann's children, a young boy that I will call "William." Though "William" is not his real name, the story that I have been guided to share with my readers is genuine.

∞

As I have previously mentioned, Mary Ann was not unlike many women who have experienced, or are experiencing, lives where a viable pregnancy does not come easily, so in 2007 all who knew Mary Ann and her husband were quite happy when she became pregnant.

In May of that year I was first given the sense from God that Mary Ann was pregnant when my husband Bob and I returned home from grocery shopping and saw her outside our home during a visit with our daughter-in-law, Amanda. It was at that very moment that I knew she was pregnant because God allowed me to feel the energy of the baby. Shortly after Mary Ann confirmed God's diagnosis with a visit to her doctor. Needless to say, Mary Ann and her husband were overjoyed!

The months progressed and so did her pregnancy but as any woman knows the real sense of having that child comes when the baby arrives on its birthday. Although I did not have any psychic or intuitive sense of a problem with Mary Ann's pregnancy I did say a few prayers asking God to keep her and her baby safe.

On November 3, 2007 I was at home doing some housework when suddenly God asked me to connect with the spirit of an unborn baby. Of course I agreed and listened intently as the baby revealed himself to be a boy and the soon-to-be-born child of Mary Ann and her husband. The baby boy spirit asked me to give his mother a message: "Tell my mother that I'll be coming on December 29 . . . December 30th . . . December 29 . . . December 30th. Tell her I will be healthy and she doesn't have to worry! I AM COMING!"

The energy I felt from that little guy was determination. I knew that there was no way Mary Ann's baby boy would be kept from reaching his mother's arms! The love that little boy's spirit already had for his mother was intense and it was obvious to me that he would help her heal, deep within her spirit's heart.

I paused to ask the baby boy's spirit if there was anything else and he said, "Yes. Tell my mother that I don't like to have my feet cold so she should always make sure that I have warm socks and good shoes or boots!" That made me chuckle to myself as I thought, "Wow, that little spirit must have had a past life in which his feet bothered him to the point he doesn't want to go through that ever again!" I promised the baby boy's spirit that I would make sure his mother got those messages and then he was gone.

In the very instant that the infant spirit left I could feel God's energy connecting with me as he gave me the sense that my daughter-in-law, Amanda, would be visiting her friend, Mary Ann, that same night. God instructed me to give the messages to Amanda and ask her to convey them to Mary Ann. I was puzzled as to "why" I couldn't simply call Mary Ann myself to give her the news but agreed to follow God's instructions.

I found Amanda in the kitchen of our basement apartment where she confirmed that she was indeed heading over to Mary Ann's house that evening. As I explained everything about the baby's spirit visit, including the dates that he had given for his birth, I saw a look of real concern in my daughter-in-law's eyes and she quickly said, "No! No, that's too early! He can't come that early or there might be health problems with the baby."

My conscious mind knew quite well what Amanda was referencing with regards to premature births yet I could not deny the knowledge that my spirit was given from God and from the baby's spirit himself. And although I did not know Mary Ann's anticipated due date from her medical doctor, I did know the information that the baby's spirit had given was quite clear and concise; that baby boy was going to be born on December 29th or December 30, 2007, come hell or high water!

Amanda explained that Mary Ann's due date was not until mid-January, specifically, January 13, 2008. That was still two weeks after the dates that the baby boy's spirit had indicated he would be born. Amanda's face still reflected the deep concern she had for her friend and the baby but I urged her to trust God and just deliver the message. She agreed and did so that evening.

I am pleased and proud to announce that little boy's spirit *did* arrive per the scheduled date that he and the Universe had agreed upon: December 30, 2007! However, it is also important to note here that Mary Ann's labor began in the early evening hours of December 29, 2007 and continued on through the night until William's birth at 5:16 a.m. CST on the morning of December 30, 2007. He weighed in at 7 pounds, and was 20 inches long. William was examined by the doctors and determined to be a very healthy baby boy!

One might wonder if William has ever given any indication that he "knew me" from the very personal spirit connection prior to his birth and the answer is no. My own observations about William are that he is a young boy who is here to bring the gift of motherhood to his mother, Mary Ann, and that most other women do not hold his interest at this time. In addition, a healthy baby brother whom I will call "Walter," joined William on Mother's Day, 2011. Their mother, Mary Ann, has undoubtedly gone through many challenges already in her quest for motherhood but my intuition tells me that her perseverance and her patience will be well rewarded as William and Walter have come here to love her unconditionally and to be the best sons they can be, as the Universe continues to challenge her, like all mothers, to grow in spirit and to lend a helping hand to other mothers from time-to-time.

For the most part I have felt that my psychic and spiritual work with the young woman that I call "Mary Ann" is complete, as she has been given the children she had hoped and prayed for as well as proof of spirit was provided by God to boost her faith and mine. Now it is up to her to stay close to our Higher Power as she navigates her own path in life and assists the Universe in guiding her precious sons towards whatever their futures hold. I wish them well and safe journey as I move forward on my path, always eager for the next amazing spirit connection!

Acknowledgements

This book was one that, like all inspired creations, had a life path of its own and seemed to flow with an ease that kept reminding me that the Universe had a hand on the steering wheel of my book project. By choosing to follow the guidance that God and angels provided to me via the innate intuition process that each of us is blessed with I found that the twists and turns that accompany any budding book project were those that I was well equipped to handle. And in the ways that I truly needed help from others, God always lit the way and I felt a great sense of gracious acceptance from the heart of my spirit within. It is both in my heart and here within my book that I wish to acknowledge some of the people who also felt and followed the urging of their personal intuitive guidance to assist me in getting this book, *"Boots on the Stairs"* out for all to read. My deepest thanks to God, angels, and this amazing universe for all it brings to my life path!

Thanks to my son, Brent S. Duncan, for taking time out of his busy life to listen to the design idea that had come to me; an idea that I knew was meant to be the cover of this book of mine. I "saw" that cover design within my mind's eye many times but did not have the expertise to create that design on a computer. My gut instincts led me to Brent as the person who, I believe, was always meant to put my cover design for this book into its Earthly form as he possessed the ability to perceive the concept that I wanted for my book's cover as well as he has the inner gifts that allowed him to create my design for the cover art. And although Brent's expertise lies mostly in the film industry, he is another person whose spirit within contains a wealth of knowledge and has a host of creative abilities that lend themselves to many diverse creative projects. My sincere thanks to you, Brent, for your part in helping my book to reach its readers! I love you and am very proud of you, son.

Shortly after I had completed my own steps to edit and to proofread the manuscript for this book I found that the Universe asked me to allow my then-sixteen-year-old granddaughter, Autumn, to read through my completed manuscript. Autumn had always expressed an interest in writing books and God had recently given me insight into Autumn's life path in which I "saw" her working hard to become an editor. Of course, that would all require her to stay focused on her education and to follow the intuitive guidance that our Higher Power would provide to her in order to complete the many steps that would bring her to that level of expertise. The sense that I garnered from God's guidance to me was that Autumn could lend another set of eyes to my manuscript and as she read it she might find some inadvertent errors that my eyes had missed during the edit and proofreading processes. That intuitive sense of mine was correct as my granddaughter immediately spotted a word that I had misspelled within the Introduction section of this book. It was a word that I know quite well but, as happens to most of us, our minds sometimes get ahead of our bodies whenever our inner selves—our spirits within—are excited about some project we are working hard to complete. It is then that mistakes sometimes occur so I appreciate Autumn's efforts to read through my manuscript and any errors, comments, or suggestions that she brought to me. Thank you, Autumn, and I wish you the best on your personal journey in becoming an editor someday! Love you, girl!

My thanks to my good friend, Maggie, who lent me her ear many times during the course of writing, editing, and in general, bringing this book to completion. Words cannot express the importance of each of us having a reliable "sounding board" person within our lives, no matter what we need to express verbally or in written form.

Thanks to my husband, Robert (Bob) Dedeker, as he, once again, offered his love, support, and encouragement throughout the process of writing, fine-tuning, and publishing *"Boots on the Stairs."* Thank you hardly seems enough; to that I add, "I LOVE you, Bob!"

Thank you and much love to any and all persons, angels, spirit guides, or spirits of the Universe who contributed to the making of this book. And a very special thanks to my son Brady's spirit for all that you have worked so hard to teach me: you are always loved and always missed! You have certainly left an indelible impression upon my spirit, mind, and body; I have no doubt that my readers will feel the same way!

About the Author

Boots on the Stairs is the fifth book written and published by psychic medium and author, Robin Jayne Dedeker. Her first book, *Moments of Intuition through Life, Love, and Loss*, was first published as an eBook in July 2010. Three years later Robin brought her first book out in print. *Moments of Intuition through Life, Love, and Loss* serves as an introduction for her readers to learn about her work as a psychic medium, as well as to help humankind to recognize, and to better understand, our innate gift of intuition by sharing stories from her own life.

As a writer, Robin is committed to educating and enlightening humankind by sharing the amazing stories of psychic and spirit connections that the Universe continues to bless her with so her readers can look forward to more books in the future!

Robin Jayne Dedeker's work as a psychic medium continues to touch the hearts and lives of any person whom the Universe places within her path. Her psychic work includes, but is not limited to: psychic readings, business intuitive consulting, private and group classes, missing persons, and ghost busting also known as spirit crossing. For more information and to see a complete listing of all of Robin's books, please go to Robin Jayne Dedeker's official website:

www.MomentsOfIntuition.com.

Robin currently lives in Shakopee, Minnesota with her husband Robert (Bob) Dedeker and their dogs, Jaden, Jax, and Lucy. She enjoys walking, movies, cooking, creating art, and spending time with her close family and friends.

About the Cover Art

Designing the interior for any book takes thought and patience as there are many details that need to be included in order to make a reader's experience as enjoyable as possible. That said, I always find that the exterior, or cover portion, of any of my books always makes itself known to me through a series of intuitive visions. These are visions that occur both at night, while I am fast asleep, as well as during my waking hours. The look and feel for the cover of *Boots on the Stairs* was no exception.

In late October 2012 I contacted my eldest son, Brent, to discuss the image that I "saw" in my mind's eye every time I thought about this particular book of mine. At that time I was not at all familiar with Adobe's Photoshop computer program, but knew that the Universe, whom I call God, had already begun to push me to begin to learn several computer programs. At first I felt rather overwhelmed, but knew that God always seems to know, better than I, the true nature and the full scope of my abilities. In any case, I felt that a good place to start would be to describe my recurring vision for the cover of my book to my son, Brent. I knew that he would be very helpful to bring my vision to its rightful Earthly place on the cover of *Boots on the Stairs*.

Brent has long had his own sense of intuitive guidance from the Universe that has allowed him to develop, and to pursue, a healthy career in films. Much like God has urged me to learn all I can about the publishing industry, so, too, has my son been brought to a place within his life path where he has knowledge of, and can personally perform, most of the tasks that are required to bring a film from a thought . . . to a tangible product that others can view in video form. In that way, the Universe appears to be making quite certain that both books and films will be left with the clear impressions of positive energy that comes through my work, and from the work of my son, Brent.

Our collaborative effort to bring my book's cover to life was not only enjoyable, but it served to further remind me of how well humans can "visualize" exactly what another person is referencing, if only we stay open to the intuitive process.

The stairs on the book's cover are, of course, a direct reference to all that I have shared with my readers within Chapter One of this book. But those stairs also symbolize the way each of us learns and grows in spiritual knowledge, one step at a time. With every life experience, including, but not limited to, spirit connections, each one of us gains spiritual insights. Through those insights we grow closer to understanding our relationship with our Higher Power and with all that the universe has to offer.

The heavens that have "opened up" represent the very nature of spirit connections and the ease at which each of us can access all that we need in our lives. I urge each of my readers to stay open to the Universe and to all of the incredible, unconditionally loving, and healing spirit connections that come your way! My sense is that you will not regret it! And with that in mind, I will end my book, but I will never end my search for spiritual understanding through God's amazing gift of spirit connections!

Available Books

The following is a current list of Robin Jayne Dedeker's books that are now available in print. Please keep in mind that she is also writing and publishing new books whenever it is time in God's universe, so for an up-to-date listing of Robin's books, please visit her Web site at:

www.MomentsOfIntuition.com

Books:

~*Moments of Intuition through Life, Love, and Loss*©

~*Insights*© (volume one of "Insights" series)

~*Insightful by Design*© (volume two of "Insights" series)

~*Insights from the Darkness*© (volume three/final installment of "Insights" series)

~*Boots on the Stairs*©

Coming soon:

~*So Many Milestones*© Copyright 2013 by Robin Jayne Dedeker; all rights reserved.

In the works:

~*Same Tree, Different Branches*© Copyright 2013 by Robin Jayne Dedeker; all rights reserved.

~In the Face of Addiction© Copyright 2013 by Robin Jayne Dedeker; all rights reserved.

CPSIA information can be obtained at www.ICGtesting.com
Printed in the USA
LVOW08s0846031114

411669LV00018BA/609/P